Where's Frank?
An Intrepid Leader, 18 Boy Scouts,
10,000 Miles in an Open Truck
by Lloyd Philip Johnson

© Copyright 2016 Lloyd Philip Johnson

ISBN 978-1-63393-239-5

Published by

 köehlerbooks™

210 60th Street
Virginia Beach, VA 23451
212-574-7939
www.koehlerbooks.com

WHERE'S FRANK?

An Intrepid Leader, 18 Boy Scouts,
10,000 Miles in an Open Truck

LLOYD PHILIP JOHNSON

VIRGINIA BEACH
CAPE CHARLES

To the memory of
the Gilberts, Curtiss and Cragg, Sr.,
who gave a combined 56 years of
inspiring leadership to boys.

PROLOGUE

THE RAIN HAD stopped by the time the truck rolled into the outskirts of Hartford, Connecticut on that July 22 morning in 1946. Canvas still covered the truck bed, stretching from the top of one slatted side rack to the other. The eighteen rain-soaked Boy Scouts underneath gradually dried out. With the sun appearing, the boys stayed on board long enough to hear from their Scoutmaster Curtiss Gilbert that it would be a twenty-minute stop.

The truck parked at the curb between the post office and a hot dog stand. With the usual excitement about a new place, the boys jumped down and scattered to explore for candy bars and other necessities, or even a post card home to Yakima, Washington. They had racked up more than four thousand miles on the odometer and had been away from home sixteen days. All in the back of the fruit truck.

By now everyone knew the routine. You'd better get back on time, because the truck would be leaving on schedule. You knew the itinerary and that Curtiss expected you to be on board as the truck left. If you didn't make it, well, sorry for you. You'd just have to catch up.

But you also knew that the truck would drive slowly down the street honking its horn. Boy Scouts would come pouring out of candy stores and run to catch the side rails, pull themselves up, and climb over. That grace period for the stragglers usually lasted a city block; then it was off to the next destination.

After driving through the city and seeing the gold leaf dome of the state capitol, the group climbed aboard, and we headed down the highway toward New Haven. At ten miles out, someone said, "Where's Frank?" Indeed, Frank Brodersen was missing. Wide-eyed, his friends looked around. Our buddy system had not worked this time. The fourteen-year-old Scout with a jaunty air about him must still be in Hartford, we thought. But why? Could he be sick? Hurt? Lost, maybe? He was usually prompt. Several guys pounded the top of the cab to get the driver, Clarence Dibert, to stop.

Curtiss got out from the cab to confirm with Lyman Bailey, his assistant Scoutmaster in the back of the truck, that Frank hadn't boarded. Porter Lombard explained he had seen Frank in the post office writing a letter to his folks. *What to do?* Frank knew the rules. Some wanted to go back to find him. We imagined ourselves in his place. Coming out to the street to find us gone! His friends, his leaders, his protection disappeared. He probably hoped they had just moved the truck around a corner.

Curtiss wrote in the journal he kept that *no one, only a small minority, that is, pitied him or wanted to go back, thinking it would be a good lesson to Frank to have to catch up with us in New York the best way he could.* We seemed sure he could. So we drove on, headed to New Haven and Yale University.

△ △ △

That story still lives in our hearts, now just seven of the eighteen Boy Scouts, First Class and up, ages fourteen to eighteen from Yakima, Washington, who covered 10,706 miles in thirty-nine days around the United States—bundled into the back of a fruit truck. Many family and friends shake their heads, wondering who would risk taking a bunch of exuberant teenage boys in an open fruit truck around the country for six weeks. How would they survive? What about accidents, illnesses, unexpected events? Isn't it against the law now to ride in an open truck? Did the Scoutmaster plan for accommodations? How could he feed so many hungry boys?

Who was this man Curtiss Gilbert? What motivated him? Why would he give such freedom to his Scouts? Did the boys really get to wander on their own at each stop? Or disappear into a city? If they didn't make it back to the truck on time, what would he do? Would he wait? But then how did he adhere to the precise schedule he promised to parents and Scout camp destinations? Did he really drive on, expecting the kid to catch up?

CHAPTER 1

The Man

LOOKING BACK AT the trip seven decades later, we survivors smile at the potential problems and laugh at the actual ones. What happened seems unreal at times, since it could never occur today. Seven of us still enjoy reliving the adventures, the freedom, the risks we took—the ones we can remember after seventy years. The saga needs to be told in part to honor the man who dared to make it all happen, Curtiss Gilbert, Scoutmaster, who with tough love gave years of his life to boys.

**Scoutmaster Curtiss Gilbert,
honored for his years of service to boys**

He became Scoutmaster of Troop 9 in 1921, less than three years after returning from combat in WWI. He finished with his death only one year after our cross-country trip at age fifty-three, October, 1947. Twenty-six years. His oldest son Cragg picked up the leadership in 1949 and led the troop for another thirty years until 1979. The Gilbert Scout record lives as a tribute to both: fifty-six total years of building the lives of young men, an incredible gift.

The cause of Curtiss' untimely death remains unknown without an autopsy. Medical speculation at the time centered on a blood clot from an old mountain-climbing injury to his leg.

Family members describe several weeks of gradual weakness, suggesting a heart attack.

What motivated the man to lead his Scouts through so many outdoor challenges? Curtiss had a determination to make boys into men that he passed on powerfully to his oldest son. His grandson Cragg, Jr. explains: .

> *After being a captain in the trenches of WWI and hearing the whining of his troops, he determined that no amount of military training could change boys into men unless they had learned self-reliance at an earlier age. Thus, he determined to start a Scout troop after the war that would prepare boys for the next war, teaching them to rely on their orientation skills, their gumption and toughness to get through hard times in the open field. It was a five-year boot camp.*

And prepare boys he did, along with his three sons, Cragg, Mark, and Bruce. His wife Anne, with two daughters Carol Anne and Marion, completed the family. He could be a drill sergeant when needed to motivate a ragtag bunch of kids to shape up and pay attention. Not averse to risk, he established many young men as mountain climbers on the rock peaks and glacier-laden volcanoes of the Cascade Mountains, instilling a love of the mountains just as he had as a young man.

This thirst for mountain adventure allegedly led a young Curtiss Gilbert, along with Clarence Truit, to climb Mt. St. Helens, hike fifty miles east through forest ridges, and ascend Mt. Adams—incredibly all in one weekend. The story lives on that they wanted to be on Admiral Byrd's expedition to the South Pole and needed to prove their mettle.

A young Curtiss Gilbert climbing with
alpenstock and hobnail boots

Starting from our camp on Mazama Ridge for Camp Muir. Note white grease paint and colored glasses

Curtiss with his scouts ready to climb to
Camp Muir, Mt. Rainer, 10,000 ft., circa 1929

Early Scout climb
with Gilbert,
year unknown

Tic[k]lish work on the snow [...]
[...]ting up for a great slide

Sliding down the snow on Mt. Rainer, circa 1944

Roped together on a glacier during an ascent of Mount Stuart in 1938, six boys started to slide. Curtiss rushed to seize the middle of the line in an attempt to stop the fall. The boys somehow escaped serious injury, but Curtiss sustained multiple severe injuries, including a dislocated shoulder and fractured sacrum, as he slid 1,000 feet down the snow and ice, bouncing over rocks until their slide stopped. His Scouts, along with a member of the Cascadian climbing club, carried him out for thirteen miles. In honor of Curtiss's work with boys and mountains, the tallest peak in the Goat Rocks Wilderness between Mount Rainier and Mount Adams now bears his name, "Curtiss Gilbert Peak."

But who was he really? How did he think of boys and risks and adventures? What experiences shaped him? Perhaps a few

extracts from his prolific letters to his future wife Anne, written
from France, can help us understand the man. An Army Captain
aged twenty-four in WWI near the end of the war, 1918, Curtiss
describes a bit of that "war to end all wars" in letters to Anne.

*The sun was shining pleasantly, and were it not for
the inferno going on all around, it would have been a
perfect autumn day. About 2:30 in the afternoon or, as
we always called it, 14:30, the order came around that
after a 5-minute artillery preparation, the attack would
be pushed on "at all cost at 15:00." That is the kind of order
that hurts, but we knew so little about what was going on
that we felt it must be the right thing to do, so responded
cheerfully. There was no artillery preparation for some
reason, so everything began to move at the prescribed
moment. Our M.G.s put down as good a barrage as they
could, but it was the reckless disregard of danger that
must have thrown those German Machine Gunners into
a panic. But as soon as the Germans saw our line after
line, or wave after wave, as they are usually called in this
war, come over the rises and hills, red lights and rockets
went up, and in response came the German barrage. It
struck the crest of the slope on which we had lain all
morning and just as we got under way. My, what a lot
of smoke, noise, and bursting shells. Bet and I sort of
worked together getting our Bu. Hq. group of about 70
men, forward. I had not gone 50 yds. when a shell struck
almost at my feet, blowing a chap who was to my left*

almost in two. My web pistol belt was nearly cut off me just opposite my right hip, and a little piece went thru the right forearm of my coat sleeve, just breaking the skin on my forearm. On we went, finally getting thru this barrage with surprising few losses. Then it was the German planes came over, and under their direction kept the barrage regulated so that it fell on us again. Our formation was so perfect and pretty, they could not help seeing it. But on we went. Cherril went ahead time and again, absolutely oblivious of danger. Several times, he found a little protection behind a terrace or hedge and would shout to me to bring the headquarters over to the right oblique. In this way we had protection thru most of the heaviest shelling. About 16:30, the order came thru that the 2nd Bu. would go thru the 362nd and occupy the front line. This order went out to the companies, and they executed it by moving up to the front line, pushing ahead beyond Gesnes and occupying the hill to the north of the town. Bu. Hq. did not keep up with the companies. It was in a series of trenches, which were almost boxed by a German barrage. Consequently, as soon as the firing diminished, Cherril went forward to reconnoiter. This was about 5:30 or 6:00 in the evening. We were getting a bit uneasy before we heard Bet's voice calling Major Ward. He had been away an hour and a half, which was too long. As Bet came to where the Major was sitting, he sank at the Major's feet in a heap. He was simply exhausted and had fainted.

I found the little shack and got a few hours sleep where the Major had spent the night before while his battalion lay scattered over the country waiting for orders. Cherril R. Betterton was the bearer of those orders. He had left our advanced units, who was then returning to the line for the front line alone, reached a part of F. Co. and secured a man named John Cudd, a corporal, to accompany him, while he made a tour of the rest of the line, notifying the different companies to return to the position of the day before. Not long after this, the corporal returned to his company in a bad state of fright and crying with grief and anger. "Lt. Betterton's been killed." He told everyone whom he met. It seemed they had been going up the hill when a voice challenged them in German. They hit the ground instantly, but a machine gun opened on them at close range. The Corporal remembers Bet's shouting, "Run for your life; I'm a goner." This the corporal did amid a rain of bullets and said it was a wonder that he could get out. The corporal had not paid much attention to where Bet had been leading him, so he could not lead anyone to the place. A week later, Lt. McLoughlin looked over this hillside quite carefully, but could find no sign of Cherril. The American dead had not been buried either, so the theory of his being wounded and taken to a German hospital developed.

Note 27 Feb. 1919:

The above is the best account of the days leading up to the 29th of Sept., which I have yet put into print.

Back home after the war, Curtiss wrote to Anne about his intense love of outdoor adventures. Returning to his beloved Cascade Mountains must have been healing for him.

July 18, 1919

Yakima, Wa

Anne Dearest,

Before I knew you so well, Anne, nature was the one thing in the world I loved most. The trails, the streams, the forests, and the mountains of the Cascades within a 90-mile radius have lured me to their vastness every summer. And to get back among them seemed like renewing old friendships, even a little as it was and will be to see you.

The boys had 60 days of intense camping. With packhorses we got into the wildest places in the mountains. Wilder than we desired at times, for there was no trail. and the swamps and fallen timber were almost impassable. No one was the least bit ill and felt so fit, they derived keen enjoyment out of the hardships. Gnats, mosquitoes, and flies at times were extremely annoying. And when it came to climbing Mount Adams [elevation 12,307 feet, author's note], why, they took it like a pack of greyhounds. I had to keep the younger ones a hold of the "lifeline" by threats, for they would have liked to take the chances that only experienced mt. climbers should take. When I went up in 1911 with the YMCA party, it took us 6 hours' climbing time, but these youngsters made it in 4 hours, and when they got to the top, they had their pictures taken standing on their heads.

Your fear of our differing is not so terrible. We love each other as much as we know how, and as long as we do that, it will heal all our differences. Remember we are to be partners. Partners in the great game of life, sticking by each other through thick and thin and merging our counsel for the benefit of the partnership. Each of us healthy and able to take care of ourselves, but hoping to make greater success by our combined efforts.

Don't work too hard. You ought to be able to walk to school every day, as far as being fit is concerned.

Write often. With sincerest love,

Curtiss

His concern about his lack of emotional response troubled him as he spoke of his background of stoicism to his future bride.

Dearest Little Girl: July 26-27, 1919

One time, Anne, you told me to come to you with things that troubled me. I am going to do it now. I have been brought up in an environment where Spartan Stoicism has been the extent of emotion or demonstrativeness. I scarcely remember kissing my Mother six times in my life. She has tried to make me express my affection for her more demonstratively, but the astuteness of the Indian has always appealed to me. The lack of emotion or sentiment I found in the army has strengthened this shell of restraint so that I guess I am or rather have made myself as unemotional as a savage. Now I find I am not as hard hearted as I thought I was and feel there is something lacking in my expression of interest in my fellow man. I had become so firmly convinced that such things as putting an arm about a sweetheart was ungentlemanly that the young lady would resent it, in fact it was with considerable misgivings that I risked it the other evening... Curtiss

CHAPTER 2

A Post-WWII Goldmine

IMAGINE JULY, 1946. WWII ended just eleven months ago with the unconditional surrender of the Japanese generals to General MacArthur on the battleship *USS Missouri*. Their collapse followed President Harry Truman's decision to drop two atomic bombs on Hiroshima and Nagasaki, respectively. We didn't question the president's decision then because it avoided the bloodbath of a Japanese invasion. The national euphoria had scarcely subsided as hundreds of thousands of American troops continued to return from both the European and Pacific theaters. Cragg, Curtiss' oldest son, had been serving in Europe with the U.S. Army 10th Mountain Division. He returned just in time to take over the orchard between the time of cherry and peach harvests. That freed Curtiss for the trip.

The Cold War with the Soviet Union began as the liberating

Russian troops entrenched themselves in Eastern Europe and Germany, causing Winston Churchill to declare "an iron curtain has descended in Europe."

But the nation shifted quickly from producing tanks and guns to making cars and civilian trucks again after five long years of driving our 1941 and older models. Among many rationed items during the war (women had no nylon stockings), gasoline seemed to head the list. Gas rationing ended August 15, 1946, just one month after our Scouting trip departure from Yakima. Fortunately, farmers remained exempt from rationing, as did other high priority occupations such as physicians, enabling us to buy gas without restriction.

△ △ △

Yakima, an agricultural town of 30,000 people in Central Washington, dozed a bit through the wartime, being safely east of the mountains from Seattle. The farm community was not affected by the blackouts from fear of Japanese bombing, as was Seattle. But Yakima did participate in the shameful roundup of ethnic Japanese citizens to the "re-location camps" in Idaho.

Irrigation systems starting from snow melt in the Cascade Mountains had converted the sagebrush desert into a flourishing valley of fruit orchards and field crops extending for many miles through the upper and lower valleys until the Yakima River plunged into the mighty Columbia near Hanford. The public didn't know until after the war that at Hanford, nuclear scientists created plutonium for the atomic bombs dropped on Japan. They were part of the secret Manhattan Project.

Growing up in rural America seemed far from any trouble. Our parents gathered world happenings from newspapers, radio, and newsreels in movie theaters. For boys, adventures beckoned.

△ △ △

By the 1940s Curtiss Gilbert, orchardist, grew apples in a large family operation. Hence, the fruit truck. Designated at one and a half tons, the chest-high bed of the truck measured nearly twenty feet long by eight feet wide. Slatted wooden sides and end provided the enclosure, all about eight feet high. He outfitted it with benches on either side, shelves in front behind the cab, and a system of poles and canvas that provided a high sleeping deck for Scouts, enabling us to travel at night if necessary. Others slept in their sleeping bags with thin mattresses on boards placed perpendicular on the side benches while driving through the night.

At one point on the journey, Curtiss described the process of putting it together:

> *Quite a crowd of natives [he probably meant local residents] watched the truck being prepared for the night run. Peterson, Porter, Mark, Sturgis, and Block did most of the work, as usual. First, the three 1 x 12 boards for filling in between the seats were put in place and covered with light mattresses that had once been used in the ski cabin back in Yakima. The canvas deck was put up about three feet above the seat mattresses. This heavy canvas was held flat and rigid by stretcher poles running from one sideboard of the truck across to the other sideboard.*

It accommodated 6 of the lighter-weight boys.

In the storage compartment above the cab, Dan McNamara and Peterson always spread their mattresses. Thus, with 9 sleeping crosswise on the seat mattresses and 9 above, 3 were left to sit in the cab, or as usually happened, Lyman or Block lay down in the back end of the truck while CRG and Clarence occupied the cab. As the decks were made ready, each one got his sleeping bag, stripped to underwear, and crawled into the 'old sock.' No one was the least embarrassed by the watching crowd.

Two other adults joined to help— Lyman Bailey, school teacher and designated assistant Scoutmaster for the trip, and Clarence Dibert, orchard warehouse manager and driver.

△ △ △

Boy Scouts from Troop 9 had raised funds for the trip with recycling paper drives through the years of WWII. By 1946, they'd raised six hundred dollars, which would pay for gasoline at less than twenty cents per gallon. Some of us younger boys received the largesse of those who worked through the war years. Curtiss's youngest son, Bruce, relates that he and sister Marion would go over the magazines collected for the paper drive, she cutting out fashion pictures and he looking for the forbidden Esquire magazines.

Ben Lombard remembers that he and two other Scouts, Bob Comer and Dick Willard, were to supply their sixty dollars for candy and goodies from their paper routes. But Dick lost his job after delivering newspapers with a hole in them. A bully had shot a hole in his stack with a .22 gauge rifle. So Curtiss offered to pay the sixty dollars for Dick if the boys collected one thousand pounds of paper for the recycling fund raiser.

Ben recalls, *We got the papers from the city public paper drive cage (it was one year after the war), and Curtiss guessed it before we could make up our own version. We were punished, and it was usually by a whack or four-hour early morning guard duty later somewhere in the wilderness.*

△ △ △

In 1937, Curtiss Gilbert took his Boy Scouts to a Jamboree in New York. Then in 1941, he took them to California twice, using his truck, to climb the volcanic mountains of the Cascades, south of the Columbia River in 1941, according to his son Bruce. So the idea of taking a bunch of Scouts around the country for nearly six weeks in the back of a truck didn't seem preposterous to Curtiss.

△ △ △

An unexpected "lost" treasure appeared in 2013, apparently known only to a few family members. Cragg "Burr" Gilbert found his grandfather's handwritten journal of the trip on a high office shelf at Gilbert Orchards. It included footnotes by Lyman Bailey "from the back of the truck." So Frank Bacon from Yakima, one of the surviving Scouts, printed Gilbert's travelogue and Bailey's notes as *The Big Trip, Troup 9, Touring U.S.A. On A Truck, July-August 1946. Notes of Curtiss R. Gilbert.* This gold mine enabled telling the story so many of us and our families have marveled at for so long.

The treasure that takes us back to post-WWII in 1946

Of the eighteen boys on the truck, only seven of us survive to remember the events after nearly seventy years. All seven of us, among other Scouts in Gilbert's account, figure in the story.

These seven still alive: Ben Lombard, Frank Bacon, Porter Lombard, Frank Brodersen, and Bruce Gilbert, noted above, join with Dick Cole and Lloyd Johnson, author of this book.

In trying to be faithful to the written journals, I have quoted extensively from the colorful accounts of our leaders, designated by italics. Some quotations are shortened, keeping the meaning. Curtiss referred to himself with his initials, CRG. Much of the fun provided by the actual writings of our leaders at the time begged to be included. Their somewhat whimsical sense of humor is timeless.

In addition, the memories of my survivor colleagues are quoted and noted similarly.

Converting a daily travelogue/diary to a coherent story of human interest accurately requires careful picking and choosing from the whole, with narrative explanations in between. Checked out with all concerned, the passages not designated as quotations are the contributions of the author, who alone should take the responsibility for any misinterpretations.

Looking back now, this adventure seems so improbable, full of risk, liability, and fun. It's a tribute to a man who cared about boys enough to put his own reputation in jeopardy. Perhaps his life. It could never happen now. But we Scouts learned that enjoying adventure in life carries risk.

The grand tour to see America around the
periphery of the continental United States, the western half

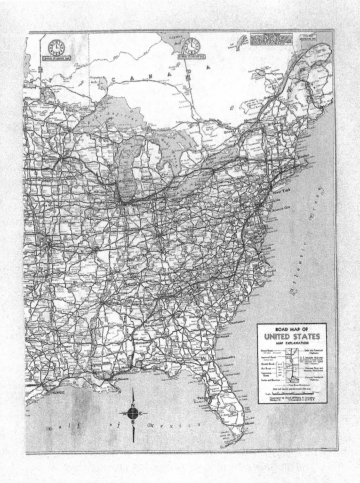

...and the eastern half

CHAPTER 3

The Grand Departure

IF CURTISS GILBERT ever had any doubts about the *Truck Trip East*, we didn't know it until we found what he wrote in his journal two months before embarking. He knew boys after so many years of leading Scouts, and he knew how they should handle themselves, whether in the city or roped up on a glacier, staring into a crevasse. A man's man, we respected him and held him in a bit of awe, but also found him friendly and personable. Ramrod straight, average height, he had a commanding voice and presence. Yet even the strongest of us have occasional questions whether we are doing the right thing.

Two months before departure, Curtiss wrote, *There will be a grand departure with the mass of detail coming to a head a few hours before departure. The truck, we hope, will be a new one, although we are willing to take a 1941 one. While it seems almost impossible to think of carrying out the plans for the trip,*

I only hope the gang does not lose patience, blow up, and head home together or in pieces.

The truck? A blue 1941 Ford.

Home away from home, a five-year-old 1941 Ford

△ △ △

With afternoon temperatures in the nineties or above in July, Curtiss decided on an evening departure. His family lived on Yakima Avenue in a modest home just west of Downtown, across the street from the large home of his parents, later to become the Gilbert Homeplace.

Sleeping bags, pear boxes standing in for suitcases, and food and clothing covered the small front yard in that early evening. Uniformed Scouts scurried around, packing and loading, the air crackling with excitement. Parents and friends filled the street in front, stopping traffic at times, probably wondering whether the chaos could ever get untangled. They had accepted that Curtiss

Gilbert could somehow pull this off despite all that could happen.

My own parents had argued about whether to let me go. My mother expressed trepidation, but their implicit trust in Curtiss, his reputation, and fame in Yakima finally won the day. Curtiss did come to our homes to reassure the families of his care for their boys' safety.

The truck and apprehensive parents

But the boys? Dressed up and ready to go

With movie cameras recording and shutters clicking, the big truck pulled out, loaded with boys hanging on the side racks waving to their disappearing parents.

July 6. We left Yakima at seven in the evening in high spirits, Curtiss wrote. Lyman's color commentary from the back of the truck explains, *Everyone sung his head off for three hours straight, exuberant as escaped chimps that had left the zoo. We exhausted most of our repertoire of songs, including the all-time favorite Sioux City Sue. I do recall the chorus, "Sioux City Sue, Sioux City Sue, your hair is red, your eyes are blue. I'd swap my horse and dawg for you."*

Lyman Bailey, a twenty-five-year-old junior high school teacher, was brought on as assistant Scoutmaster for the trip. He seemed to know every song, operatic aria, and Gilbert and Sullivan lyric. Small, slightly built, single, and effervescent, with Coke-bottle glasses, he couldn't be more different from Curtiss. Despite his artistic temperament and sensitivity, he would make every effort to bridge the gap with a bunch of exuberant outdoor guys. His colorful notes traveling with us in back contrast with Gilbert's sometimes cryptic statements of fact. Curtiss rode in the cab with Clarence Dibert, oftentimes driving, occasionally hosting one of the boys there if injured or needed for navigation.

After the desert of sagebrush hills, we arrived at Vantage along the Columbia River and changed out of our uniforms before all heading to a soft drink stand, which comprised the whole place—except for a nearby petrified forest. Then across the bridge we drove toward Spokane through the irrigated Columbia Basin with its range and farmland, scattered houses, and few trees.

At another stop for sodas, we learned of a lake up ahead. We never questioned where we would stay for the night, assuming Curtiss had it all planned. But not so, as his journal entry shows: *A side road led to the lake, but instead of a good campsite for a group of tired travelers, we found a dance pavilion with hundreds of people.*

The music and crowd attracted our curiosity, but would not be good for getting a night's sleep. We had trouble turning the truck around in the crowded parking lot, but finally headed back to the highway and into the unknown, with no idea where to camp. It had been a long and exciting day, but the adrenalin rush faded to fatigue. Finally, after midnight, our senior patrol leader (SPL) Ted Block, who was riding up front with his flashlight, spotted a road leading to a grassy parklike area with pine trees. Curtiss suggested his relief at finally locating a suitable campsite at 12:30. *In a moment, a gate was down, and the truck was parked a discreet distance from the main highway. . . . In a few minutes twinkling lights marked the groups as the boys set up tents or unrolled bedrolls. It was difficult getting everything quiet.* Only in the morning could we see where we were: out in the middle of vast expanses of land with grasses, sagebrush, and a distant farmhouse with outbuildings.

That became the pattern— finding some camping site, not

worrying too much about what the local farmers thought. But taking care to keep the site clean. Our Scout leader did try to keep noise down and leave early in the morning to avoid trouble from ranchers wondering what group of ruffians had invaded their land.

By four in the morning, Curtiss was getting the K.P.s (kitchen police) up for breakfast. We had gas stoves and water, but not much sleep, leaving before any farmers could get curious.

△ △ △

Nearing Sand Point, Idaho, Curtiss wrote, *Several bloody noses were received by over-spirited boys in the back of the truck. Bacon and Block staged a good bout.*

But Lyman from the back of the truck provided the details.

"This was the greatest Battle Royal I was to witness on the whole trip. Only the more pacific were spared. All were drawn into one grand free-for-all, mostly 2 or 3 smaller boys ganging up (in good spirits—just to see if they could actually bulldog the larger fellow) on Bob Peterson, Ted Block, Mark Gilbert, and Dan McNamara. The boys thought it interesting to observe also 'who got mad.' This was definitely considered poor taste: to 'get mad' when assailed and your nose bloodied by the smaller fry. Bob Comer, Frank Bacon, and Ben Lombard led the assault."

These contests reflected the usual practice of ending our Scout meetings in the basement of the church with the lights suddenly going out and a free-for-all roughhouse with anybody we encountered in the dark. So Lyman's description caught the spirit of the thing and the importance of not getting mad.

△ △ △

Frank Bacon with others led the assault that day. At age fourteen, he gave ground to no one, a future stellar high school football player. His family had recently moved to Yakima. He joined the troop one year before the trip and climbed to the 14,408-foot summit of Mount Rainier along with Curtiss Gilbert, at age thirteen the youngest boy to have summited at that time. Curtiss sometimes referred to him in his journal as just "Bacon" to distinguish him from Frank Brodersen, the Scout we left behind in Hartford whose absence someone announced with, "Where's Frank?"

Ben Lombard, younger brother of Porter and also among our seven survivors, played a fun role on the excursion, often doing crazy things, sometimes in trouble along with the rest of us, other times alone. As one of the younger boys, he also started the first rumble in the truck along with Bacon and Bob Comer. Curtiss Gilbert had taught Ben in Sunday school at the Congregational Church.

Ben had also climbed Mount Rainier with Bacon the year before, with Curtiss in the lead. But Ben, as part of the fourth rope team led by a young experienced climber Jim Malcolm, lagged behind because two partners could not keep up the pace. He dropped out while the teams well ahead continued their ascent. Ben and Malcolm unselfishly stayed in place to watch their tired partners safely return to base camp at ten thousand feet. They missed the clear weather on the mountain, became enveloped in fog and sixty-mile-an-hour freezing wind near the top, and lost their way. They did eventually summit by midafternoon, "crawling on hands and knees," Ben relates. But descending with fog and crevasses, they lost their footing, exhausted, and slid down the glacier in the soft afternoon snow almost into a crevasse. The others climbed back up to rescue them, as they wisely remained where they ended their fall.

CHAPTER 4

Montana Mud

ON TO KALISPELL, Montana, and groceries. We approached spectacular Glacier National Park in rain showers, having covered 526 miles from home. Camped on the shore of Lake McDonald in a public campground this time, we watched the other rain-soaked campers pack up and leave. But with mountain tents and canvas, our group stayed dry through the night.

Stopping for a break after the rains

The next morning, we were up at six in the rain. It was July 8, and our Scoutmaster wrote, "[David] Acton (quartermaster) was the one to be on the job first." Wet but hungry, we probably agreed with Curtiss that the "menu of canned prunes, mush, eggs, and ham was excellent."

Pausing at Lake McDonald Post Office and
General Store near Glacier National Park

The mountain scenery with peaks, glaciers, and wildflowers impressed Curtiss. Having climbed on mountain glaciers, some of us took the beauty of the park for granted. We stopped at Logan Pass to fill the refrigerator with snow.

Later we stopped at the *big, ritzy Many Glacier Hotel. Curtiss had not intended to stop, but realizing the boys lived in a democracy where all are supposed to be equal, they [we] risked being thrown out, parked among Cadillacs, and strolled into the high-priced hotel. It was hard to get the boys away.*

△ △ △

At Fairfield, Montana, a flat tire required a new inner tube, and we lost an hour and a half putting it on. Curtiss made many entries lamenting delays and events like tire blowouts that fouled up his schedule. Crossing the Missouri River heading for Great Falls Park, it rained and blew all night. Supper finished at ten-thirty, and boys slept either in tents or under canvas on the gravel road at the fish hatchery park. Except that "Bob Comer stayed in the cab of the truck." Curtiss usually had sick or injured boys ride or sleep up front.

Lyman describes it as, *A miserable night. Some introduction to our Grand Tour! And the time it took for a meal! Most of us might many times have crept exhausted to rest without struggling with stove and lamps except for Curtiss, the Indomitable, refusing to let a mere flood and gust of wind and no shelter daunt him.*

Up at four-thirty on July 9, the boys cooked mush under canvas wind shelters. Several were very wet. Lyman wrote, *What a waster of time the human meal is. It seemed like each individual's motions had to be coaxed along by a Higher Authority, and things dragged along like a nightmare. Maybe we were groggy from no sleep. Hot cocoa does taste good on a fresh morning after a rain, tho!*

△ △ △

We tried to find the falls on the Missouri River that Lewis and Clark detoured eighteen miles around carrying their equipment. At each historical marker Ken Sturgis would shout, *"Quiet, everybody, here's another Hysterical Point."* Curtiss laments, *Got onto a little dirt road, and the rain had made it so muddy, we almost got stuck in the first 50 feet.*

Lyman sheds more light: *Our swarm of pygmies pushing with slippery, ever-muddier shoes, in the sopping wet, with the truck wheels spinning, a shovelful or two of gravel or grass thrown under in frenzy every few moments by a small, sweating gang. The great blue behemoth actually moved! What a shout went up when we finally crept to the top—like a drowned crew being saved from perdition!*

Curtiss continues: *Nearly 2 hours had been wasted before we got back to Great Falls. Then we were so rattled, we headed back the road we had come in on the night before for about 5 miles. So it was nearly 10 o'clock before we turned toward Helena, but the boys were singing lustily, "High, high up she rises!"*

Lyman notes, *We have nothing but black contempt and hatred for Montana mud. In fact, we made up a derisive battle song about it. The hi up she rises song was one of our finest vocal attempts . . . (improvising words like Ted Block's "Give him some boys and let him boss'em.")* Appropriate for the senior patrol leader, who with his booming voice exercised his authority loud and often. *This went on for about 20 miles and made us forget the misery of wet and mud,* Lyman concluded.

Lewis and Clark's falls on the Missouri River never crossed our retinas. We were just glad to get out of there.

Looks a little chaotic, not sure where or who's on the floor

CHAPTER 5

Mosquitoes

LYMAN SHARED A bit of the man while at Yellowstone's Mammoth Hot Springs: *Here was one of the opportunities to see Curtiss's way with boys by direct talk. I remember his reassurances to the young ones that they weren't missing anything by not going to the lodge (just a place to spend money), and partly suggesting and kidding, getting Ben and others to use the time to write notes home. When making and breaking camp, Curtiss was a sort of an induction–motor who did much himself, all the while stirring the boys around him with: 'who's taking care of the'—he himself with hands full of hard jobs, the skilled labor, and the hard job of boy management.*

July 10. After taking moose pictures and Old Faithful shots, we arrived at Old Faithful Inn four days out. The boys took in the big indoor swimming pool. Lyman writes, *It was our best opportunity to get clean and feel human for a week or so. How they loved bobbing around in these warm waters and playing games.* You wonder who enjoyed "getting clean" the most.

Curtiss sent a telegram from Old Faithful Inn, saying: *All well. Behind schedule one day account rain. Glacier, Yellowstone perfect.* Then after watching Old Faithful active for its three-minute spectacle, Curtiss writes, *After waiting for Brodersen, it was 3:45 before we could get going.*

Frank Brodersen explains, *I was stuck in the back of our group and couldn't see the eruption. Damned if I was going to miss seeing it, so I stayed until it went off again.* Frank, one of the younger boys, had more adventures with schedules, but it didn't dampen his enthusiasm. He actually lived in Oregon, but his family had connections with Yakima, the troop, and the Congregational Church, so he came along, but didn't know any boys at first. His parents had driven him from Forest Grove just in time to board the truck. *When the blue truck arrived, Curtiss handed me a box and said, "Here, put your clothes in this box; we're not taking suitcases." I was also told that he'd assigned Ben Lombard and me to be responsible for each other; we were to check to see if we were on the truck before it left after a stop. Those two instructions were my introduction to the trip.*

I was not quite 15, weighed about 110 lbs. and would quantify myself as louder than necessary, above-average student, not much of an athlete, but played high school baseball.

△ △ △

Between waiting for late kids and numerous flat tires, Curtiss's angst over keeping to the advertised schedule comes out in his journal. And he did levy fines for being late: one cent for every minute not present. It diminished slightly our sixty-dollar stash for ice cream, but we generally accepted our punishment as justice administered.

July 11. Camped among mosquitoes at String Lake in the shadow of the Grand Tetons, our intrepid Scoutmaster got everyone up at five for a breakfast of prunes, Farina, and cocoa. Back north to Yellowstone, Bruce Gilbert found his lost sunglasses, and Dave Acton fished while the rest of us visited spectacular Yellowstone Canyon and Falls. Acton caught nothing. But Curtiss noted Lyman found four excellent pies.

David Acton worked hard as quartermaster; a bit older than us younger Scouts, he was funny often in his frustration to get some of us to help in the kitchen duties. Usually, he rose before the rest of us struggled out of our sleeping bags in the early morning hours. Feeding eighteen hungry boys and three adults had to involve much planning, buying, preparing, and serving. As chief cook and food manager, he contributed much, but I don't recall that we ever told him so.

Bruce Gilbert, Curtiss's youngest son and one of our surviving troop members, had become a very special friend. He would do anything for you. Somewhat quiet and even shy, particularly with girls, Bruce had his own mind, a determined set of goals, and great humor not hidden to his close friends. We often tented together when others slept out in the open, sometimes plagued by bugs. On a later mountain trip he rose in the night into the cold driving rain outside the tent to find something I needed to catch my vomit.

△ △ △

Cody, Wyoming, full of Buffalo Bill memories, afforded an opportunity to get the truck serviced. Curtiss notes, *We started for Sheridan at 5:20 p.m. Eleven miles out on the rolling range, the engine sputtered and stopped. We realized we had not gotten gas at Cody. A couple from Indiana had met some of the boys in Cody, and they offered to sell some gas if we had a hose to siphon it out of their tank. At last we thought of the little vacuum hose on the windshield swipes and in due course of time had four gallons transferred to our can and thence to our tank. We lost over an hour, but we were lucky we did not have to go back to Cody.*

This Granite Pass climb (on the way to Sheridan, Wyoming) *was one of the longest 2 hours I remember on the trip,* Lyman noted. *The truck grinding along in low, the roughness, steepness, and serpentine nature of the mountain road, the coolness increasing, the uncertainty. We finally achieved the summit.*

Curtiss the climber kept accurate elevation records, ascending from 4183 to 8950 feet.

△ △ △

July 12. Finding a city park in Sheridan after midnight. Curtiss the indomitable caved in to misery and felt sorry for us. *The mosquitoes were so bad, we rolled out at 4:20 a.m. without any more than washing up at the Shell station.* Even he had his limits for bugs. *We took off for any place where there were fewer mosquitoes.*

One was at Devil's Tower National Monument, Wyoming, where the jealous rock climbers of the group watched two men ascend the sheer cliff wall using pitons. The perilous final cliffs added to their excitement.

Porter Lombard was among those of us watching. In contrast to his younger brother Ben, he seemed to have a quiet, adventurous spirit that came out at various times. Curtiss inspired Porter at Sunday school teaching with stories and before the big trip had led Porter and others on an excursion to the Snake River and a climb of the Oregon Matterhorn.

CHAPTER 6

First Casualty

THE LONG DAY ended in South Dakota, searching a public campground with flashlights to find an unoccupied fireplace. We at least had found a campground. Stretching our days traveling in the truck at around forty-five miles per hour, none of us can now recall how we spent the hours—except when something unusual happened. Probably lots of watching of scenes flowing by, talking, playing games. But we kept to schedule most of the time, which required pushing on to the planned destination in spite of the approach of night. Porter Lombard, amazed at the flat landscape of the Midwest, noted he could see lights of distant cities thirty miles away, so unlike home. The late arrival times meant hungry and tired boys cooking and setting up camp in the dark. That made for some concern, particularly when the kitchen preparation bogged down.

Most of us had no idea what was wrong that night. Curtiss commented, *"It was nearly 11 before we ate, and the rice had not cooked even then."* So what to do with starving stomachs late at night with no way to cook the staple?

Here Lyman chimes in, *Bailey had one chance to be useful. In the confusing nocturnal scuffle with cooking apparatus, the needle valve for the gas stove got lost on the ground. Everybody hunted. No success. Then Bailey (fanfare of trumpets) with his little myopic eyes and thick lenses gets down to paw thru the leaves, and with systematic perseverance he finally locates the small nut, and the battle with uncooked rice can proceed. Triumph!*

Curtiss shrugs, *Either in tents or on canvas to avoid poison ivy, we unrolled our sleeping bags.*

△ △ △

July 13. The scaffolding still up didn't hide the huge busts carved into the white granite vein in the cliffs at Mount Rushmore National Memorial, South Dakota. High up on the precipices above us, carved into the rock, we gazed at the sixty-foot sculptures of four presidents: George Washington, Thomas Jefferson, Theodore Roosevelt, and Abraham Lincoln.

**Impressive busts of the four Presidents carved
in the granite at Mt. Rushmore**

Sculpted by Danish-American Gutzon Borglum and finished by his son Lincoln Borglum between 1927 and 1941, the impressive work strikes admiration, even in a teenage boy, of both the famous presidents and the two Borglums chipping away at the rock. The picture remains in memory. So many images do, particularly of events or places that impressed us at the time even though we took much for granted. Looking back, I realize that all the time, Curtiss had in mind the sites that would help us appreciate the country that first tried a *government of the people*. And the great men who had the vision to make that grand experiment work.

△ △ △

Then east to the Great Plains, the Badlands, and beyond, we hurried past Pierre, the state capital. Curtiss adds, *We stopped at Phillip for usual desert refreshments, but eat lunch of peanut butter, lettuce, spam, and tuna sandwiches and potato salad on truck. We lost an hour because we had to change from Mountain to Central time on the plains, where we averaged 40 miles an hour. Acton's hat blew off because he stood up too fast.* The journal doesn't tell whether we stopped to get it, but Curtiss probably did, or he wouldn't have even known it riding in the cab up front.

Going on to Doland, the boys purchased hamburgers while we put up the canvas and put the mattresses on the seats so everyone could sleep in the truck. That summarized it for Curtiss.

But now the description from our myopic leader who rescued the rice tells us what putting up the canvas really meant. *Such a tugging and a hauling (and words under breaths), and attempts to get the stubborn crosspieces thru the canvas with every tool and all hands available. Curtiss and our big stalwarts doing the work, as usual, with lots of advice: "Now shove harder, push harder." How it was finally managed, I'm not sure. The relief in having these ingenious bunks put up and the congestion relieved downstairs was heavenly, though, and made us feel quite snug and domestic—a little condensed version of the Pullman sleeper.*

Lyman wrote, *The mosquitoes compelled Curtiss and Clarence to drive all night with Scouts sleeping soundly in the truck. Everywhere they tried to stop, more mosquitoes. Going on through the wee hours. Covered 573 miles in one 24-hour period, 50 mph with no interstate highways! There was certainly no rest with them* (mosquitoes) *around.*

△ △ △

The third adult on the trip, the quiet Clarence Dibert, seemed never to tire as the designated driver. Dark hair, medium build, an employee of Gilbert Orchards, he was just there all the time. We never doubted our safety as he and Curtiss alternated driving all night long and with little sleep.

But trouble brewed. First a thunderstorm heading into Clark, South Dakota, a town near the Minnesota border. *With the boys tucked away in their sleeping bags and the flashes of lightning brightening the countryside, we were a wild busload of Scouts, splashing over wet pavement and passing blinding headlights,* Curtiss mused from the cab of the truck.

Frank Brodersen describes traveling in the back: *For night travel, I was assigned the most rear bunk in the double-deck sleeping arrangement. It felt like sleeping on the end of a diving board when the blue truck would bounce on rough pavement. However, it must not have bothered me too much, I have no memory of the brief stops made by the drivers so they could nap. However, watching the lightning storm in South Dakota from the bouncing bunk has stayed with me.*

Curtiss continues, *While Clarence drove around* (Clark, S.D.), *Ted Block, Lyman B, and CRG went with Bob Peterson, a big strong baseball pitcher at Yakima High School, up to a Dr. Christianson's office. He cleaned and dressed Pete's knee, as well as having a shot of anti-tetanus in the hip. The doctor strongly advised seeing a doctor in Minneapolis, as there were signs of infection.* Pete had fallen while hauling himself up into the truck when the rope he had grabbed broke. We were moving slowly down the street at the time. He skinned one knee severely.

Moving on, Curtiss comments, *We shoved Pete and his stiff knee into his upper sleeping berth. On and on we rolled, showers making everything glisten. At 2 a.m. we stopped on the outskirts of a village, but the mosquitoes were so bad we had to start moving. With Clarence and Curtiss changing off, 573 miles driven in 24 hours, when we stopped at 8 for gas outside Minneapolis.*

Frank Brodersen recalls arriving after that all-night drive: *In Minneapolis (I think), I have this memory of someone who'd been there before giving the driver directions. He hollered into the intercom, "Take a left right turn here...yeah, that's right." Gales of laughter greeted those instructions.*

Searching succeeded. Curtiss relates, *Ted Block and Lyman took Pete in* (to a hospital) *while we kept quiet in a little park across the street. CRG was called in to help make out a questionnaire, the life history of Bob Peterson. The doctor's verdict was hospitalization for blood poisoning in his knee, and for cure: a liberal use of the new penicillin to fight the infection. Bob drew enough money to buy a railroad ticket to New York, where he could catch up with us. And so we bid Bob goodbye in Minneapolis, he waving to us from his wardroom on the second floor . . . as we rolled away.*

Some of the Scouts felt a bit of concern at leaving one of our senior members of the troop behind, ill and hospitalized. We had no real idea when and where he would catch up. Tall and friendly, his stature as an important pitcher for Yakima High School elevated his reputation among us. Pete's humility and kindness and his hard work, for example, in assembling the upper sleeping deck would be missed. It would be the first of several absences as we left others behind, not always for good reasons like this one.

CHAPTER 7

Short Nights and Early Mornings

AFTER TOURING THE University of Minnesota and State Fairgrounds in Minneapolis, we drove to Rochester, Minnesota, the location of St. Mary's Hospital and the famous clinic. Lyman adds a footnote. *Coming to the Mayo Clinic offered embryonic Doc Johnson an opportunity to tell the story of the Mayo Bros.—Uncle Will and Uncle Charlie and their long struggle in Rochester and excellence in their profession.*

While not recalling this episode, because of my dad, a family physician in Yakima, I seemed pegged by the troop to follow in his footsteps. I do remember reading the book about the Mayo brothers, who, along with my father, became my heroes. Just another kid who loved to play, hike, ski, and swim, the trip provided me at age fourteen a welcome respite from a summer working in orchards thinning apples. A good friend of Bruce

Gilbert, I had been persuaded by him to transfer to Troop 9 from another one, for which I am eternally grateful.

△ △ △

Driving into Wisconsin, the group found a grassy unfenced field with shade, according to Curtiss, "*and soon had the gas stoves cooking fried potatoes, asparagus, ham, and pudding. The boys found a swimming hole in the creek and could hardly be persuaded to come to their meal. Then an evening drive until coming to a side road, we found a place where Ted Block, Clarence Dibert, and CRG could roll out their sleeping bags for a few hours.*" Past midnight. All the rest of us were presumably long gone in our Pullman sleepers. Once asleep in the truck as we drove, we accumulated more hours of rest than our leaders in the cab. They often had to stop in the short hours of the early morning for at least a catnap. With so little sleep, we could easily have come to grief on the highways. But while we didn't, the lack of sleep had to have taken its toll on the drivers.

July 15. Everyone was aroused and ordered to pack up so that a move could be made, because there was no water to prepare breakfast with, our Scoutmaster explained. But ten miles farther on, at the Tower Park near Spring Green, Wisconsin, *was ideal for preparing breakfast, and the boys got to see the shot tower where melted lead was dropped 100 feet and thus was broken up into shot and cooled before it hit the bottom. Breakfast was French toast and mush.*

After touring Madison, the university, the state capitol

grounds, and then Milwaukee, we headed south along Lake Michigan to Racine, Wisconsin. Another flat tire. That enabled the Scouts to get chocolate milk for seven cents per pint and write postcards. Another hour-and-a-half delay, while Curtiss and Clarence changed the tire.

△ △ △

Then down the Lake Shore Drive to the Naval Training Station and Dick Rothe's aunt's house. From there, navigating to Chicago's weekend Boy Scout camp proved difficult. When we finally arrived, the caretaker opened the gate, but food took precedence beyond a roof over our heads. Curtiss, never one for luxuries, noted, *We decided to bed down in the field rather than trouble with buildings or tent houses. At ten-thirty—canned soup, beans, bread, and pears. Mosquitoes were noticeable.*

July 16. Ten days out from Yakima, Curtiss writes, *Up at 5:15 a.m. Hard to get the boys up. Breakfast held up until 9:20.* That's the short version.

Envision what happened. Our senior patrol leader, Ted Block, wanders around a collection of sleeping bags on the ground, some with heads visible, no one stirring. His strident bass voice almost commands the dawn. But the bags don't move. He raises his voice to a higher pitch, imploring the impossible. He hears "go away" and less civilized replies. The troops rebel, and he reports to the captain who cannot admit to exhaustion himself, but relents. Costly for time and schedule. How can we tour Chicago in one day, starting when only half of its daylight remains?

△ △ △

Striking the Lake Shore Drive, our simple truck was quite lost on the six-lane highway. It's hard to imagine what all the Chicagoans thought, seeing a large fruit truck lumbering down the freeway filled with kids in the back, climbing up the side rails for a better look. We kept to the outside lane so we could stop to view the waterfront or skyline.

Lyman explains Curtiss's "simple truck." *I liked our adjustable philosophy on the Blue Truck. When the sign said "No Trucks," then we were a bus. When it was plain that "No Busses Allowed,"— you guessed it, we were a truck again. But nobody molested us, even though a time or two the leaders were a bit apprehensive at the approach of Officialdom with and without sirens.*

Clarence drove well in spite of the new traffic signals and many backseat drivers shouting over the interphone, Lyman adds, this time from the cab. *Some of Clarence's remarks on the backseat drivers on the interphone were interesting, coming from such a mild and calm individual. Suffice it to say, he didn't think them too helpful at times, usually...when he needed them the most.*

Then it was off to the Field Museum. Ben recalls now, *mummies scared the s____ out of us.*

Chicago skyline, Lake Michigan, and Curtiss with several Scouts

Clarence, along with Curtiss and Bruce, toured the stockyards where Curtiss mentioned the high mortality rate for steers—one hundred fifty animals per hour. Dick Cole and Frank Brodersen went to see a ball game. Major league baseball proved a great treat for boys from a small town.

Dick Cole, one of the younger Scouts and a survivor now, excelled later in high school baseball and skiing and became an Eagle Scout. His father, who had contacts with Curtiss at remote ski cabins near Mount Rainier, had arranged for Dick to go with us on the trip, since he belonged to another Scout troop in Yakima. Dick never felt like an outsider on the trip.

Ben and Porter Lombard took the train to Monroe, Michigan, to visit an uncle; they'd catch up in Detroit. Porter Lombard, older brother of Ben, proved different from his younger exuberant brother in manner—thoughtful, mature, quiet, and also an enthusiastic mountain climber. Porter and Bruce Gilbert had also become close friends, with their families both participating in the Congregational Church in Yakima.

After downtown and supper, Bruce and Dick Willard were twenty-five minutes late getting back to the truck. They were fined a cent a minute. The boys must have wandered off from Curtiss after dinner. Looking back, it's clear that Curtiss allowed his charges the freedom to scatter and explore. He let us take the train to other cities or into Chicago or New York without apparent concern that we would get lost, face threats, get injured, or do something stupid. He trusted us to behave and use our heads and not get lost while returning to find the truck. Amazingly, it worked—most of the time. Freedom meant adventure, admittedly with risks Curtiss accepted and most of us didn't even think about at the time.

We encountered heavy traffic getting out of Chicago. Stopped at South Bend, Indiana, for white gas for stoves. All night we drove, passing several well-lighted places and villages until four-fifteen while the Scouts slept in back. We finally dodged into a private side road, and the drivers rolled up under a big tree.

CHAPTER 8

Niagara Falls and Reunion

JULY 17. SHORT NIGHT for the drivers who were up at seven-fifteen. We took down the bunks and hit the road before stopping at a park in Ann Arbor close to the University of Michigan for cooking breakfast. Then off to Detroit and the Ford Motor Company, where we were given a young lady for a guide. Bailey expands just a bit: *The Greenfield Village young lady caused quite a bit of ribbing for our gallant young McNamara.* Unfortunately, we're not told what really happened. But so much to see—Edison's laboratory, the Wright brothers' shop, Ford's first workshop, and the chair in which Abraham Lincoln was sitting when assassinated.

After crossing the St. Clair River into Canada, the team visited Sarnia, Ontario, where Curtiss' older daughter, Marion, had settled two years previously with her Canadian husband, Clary Mann.

Mark Gilbert, Clary Mann, Marion Mann, Bruce and Curtiss Gilbert

Marion prepared the meal, a chicken dinner with potato salad, and ice cream and cake and milk were served on the back lawn as mosquitoes circled and bit.

**With Curtiss as photographer, in Sarnia,
this is our only picture of Lyman Bailey, third from left, second row.**

After some baths and shaves the boys wrote postcards home. Then they escorted us to a municipal dance hall, where everyone spread out his bed roll on the lawn.

Marion later remembered her father Curtiss had said that the meal she prepared for over twenty famished men and boys had been pretty good for a young woman. It was a rare compliment from her father, one she treasured. She couldn't know it, but when he left the next morning, she would never see him again.

△ △ △

July 18. Clarence arose at 4:30 a.m., beating CRG for the first time—due to mosquitoes. Probably hard for the boss to admit in his own notes, but honest and perhaps written with a wry smile. It wouldn't have jibed with his Spartan mindset.

Traveling on to Niagara Falls, Curtiss added, *At 5 p.m., we drove along the Canadian side of the Niagara River to see the Horseshoe Falls. A beautiful rainbow hung in the mist rising from the foot of the falls. Crossing the new bridge to the American side, we drove around the city and phoned the Scout office for directions to their weekend camp. Then good news: Ted Block had phoned to relatives in Buffalo, and they came out to the camp with Bob Peterson, who had come from Minneapolis as soon as the doctors would allow.*

Lyman commented, *The glad outcry that met Bob P. for his reunion with us was certainly a heartwarming proceeding. All the boys had to swarm about and find out in detail how he had fared with doctors, pretty nurses, drugs, germs, railroads, and all.*

Curtiss continued, *After 10 o'clock supper, we rolled out in the grass for sweet night's sleep at 11:30. Bob Peterson enjoyed his old bunk on a mattress above the truck cab.* Pete had returned, so all was well at the moment.

△ △ △

July 19. We rose early to see Niagara Falls from the American side. No more Lyman Bailey notes from the back of the truck from here on. Apparently, he did write more, according to Curtiss's journal. We'll miss the commentary, but learn what he's thinking from subsequent adventures. Curtiss relates, *Clarence arranged for servicing the truck while we took the 90-cent excursion on the little Canadian steamer, 'Maid of the Mist.'*

Maid of the Mist excursion boat in Niagara River below the falls

Scouts boarding the boat.

"In oilskin slickers the boys looked very adventurous," Curtiss noted.

Bruce took in the Cave of the Winds, and others hiked out on Goat Island to get a close-up of the American Falls.

Bruce marched to his own drum, and it often served him well, except when he forgot something important like a camera. Curtiss continues, *A delay of 2 hours was endured because of a misunderstanding by Clarence as to where we were to meet after the truck was serviced. But by 3:30 p.m., we were away.* Another snafu and time delay, duly noted in our leader's notes, like being tardy to school.

△ △ △

Buffalo and Rochester slipped by without much comment. Passing lakes, we couldn't find a non-fenced place to spend the night. But while stopping at Auburn, New York, for gasoline, a thunderstorm hit, which drenched those who took the most active part in putting up the canvas. Before leaving, everyone had gotten a hamburger, and at 11, all were tucked in bed in the back and the truck resumed its journey toward Albany. Another night drive.

On a side road the drivers stopped at 4 a.m. for a nap in a meadow, July 20, but are up and away at 7:00. A flat tire forced us to stop at a country service station for air. The boys sailed into the sleepy place, buying nearly everything edible.

At a midmorning stop for breakfast, the boys washed themselves and clothing in a polluted stream, which no one curiously but Lyman was allowed to swim in. Our leader went on without explanation, *At 11:30, punched on to a service station where a tube was repaired and a tire changed. Boys take on more pop, ice cream, etc. Ben Lombard put 30 sticks of gum in his mouth at one time.*

CHAPTER 9

New England and a Lost Boy

OVER THE APPALACHIANS, the man of pure mountain water wrote, *Streams dammed up for power and drinking water, and what little does run at this season of the year resembles a sewer. Everyone marveled how peaceable everything was about the truck. The explanation was that Ben Lombard had ridden in the front seat the night before, and, having slept very little, he had to sleep most of the day.*

In Concord, Massachusetts, he journaled, *We walked across the bridge and looked back on the countryside where the early colonists had fired on the British and then on to Lexington and the numerous statues with tales of 'the shot heard around the world;' how the first casualties had been suffered here in the Revolution; and how the colonists had been driven back to Concord before they rallied and harassed the English all the way back to Boston.*

△ △ △

Finding Boy Scout Camp Ten outside Boston, our Scoutmaster observed, *Some of the Boston–accented boys stayed up after midnight, listening to Sturgis, McNamara, and Acton.*

For the first time we began to feel the differences between our western U.S. small town culture in Yakima and historic New England with its nearly two-hundred-year history of being the original thirteen colonies resisting a foreign power. We began to realize the distance between a small country town out West, with a history of less than one hundred years, and historic New England. The Boston Scouts seemed as fascinated by our Western accents as we were hearing "Bostonese." You don't park the car; you "pak the caa."

For the first time for many of us, the world became bigger than just Yakima. At the same time we realized we are also part of that history and could take pride that those Minutemen stood behind trees, like Native Americans had done, and turned the regimented British soldiers back to Boston and their ships.

△ △ △

July 21. From the Boston Scout camp Gilbert wrote, *A hoped-for swim in the dry swimming pool abandoned because of the recent water shortage. CRG missed witnessing the big Tarzan Act—the boys doing a daredevil rope swing from the cliffs in camp—Bob Comer the only casualty with a banged foot.*

We drove into town and among the buildings of Harvard College, explaining to a cop who was about to throw us out that we were from Washington. Curtiss mentions Harvard's founding in 1636; he tried to educate us about the significance of these historic institutions. After Massachusetts Institute of Technology and Bunker Hill, we visited Old Ironsides, the U.S. Frigate *Constitution*, and the Old North Church.

All this touring in Boston took time, and to compound the problem of keeping to the schedule, we got lost. The streets became narrow with no apparent outlet. Then somehow we turned into a street that seemed to our frustrated captain like a "foreign" section of the city, maybe "Jewish or Italian." Curtiss describes it briefly: *We unintentionally got into a religious parade with a life-sized statue of Mary being carried on the shoulders of eight men at the head of the 200-odd worshippers and a 16-piece brass band bringing up the rear.* The street narrow with cars parked on the sides in places, people with children standing to see the parade—no possibility of turning around. The band played on as we joined the festivities, crawling forward, bringing up the rear of the parade, inadvertent participants with our steaming boss held in check by his stoic nature. He wrote, *Our big truck slowly ground along just behind them, and it was with much relief that we saw the statue finally turn into the front door of a church, leaving us unescorted by the rather seedy little band.*

Curtiss didn't seem to think very highly of the band or providing the great backup to the parade as it inched forward. The fascination of the people along the street pointing, laughing, and waving at the big blue truck filled with boys, contrasted with our Scoutmaster looking at his watch and about to explode. When we finally could move to the next venue, he seemed to take it out on the stream, writing, *from the old North Church where Paul Revere had seen the lanterns from across the smelly old river, we drove down the coast toward Plymouth Rock.*

△ △ △

Where the Pilgrims landed, Curtiss added, *the boys spied a popcorn wagon and ran for refreshment. There were two men dressed as Puritans walking about the edifice.*

"Why," Bob Comer asked, "are you dressed up like that?"

"We missed the boat and are waiting for them to come back and get us."

Porter Lombard got a lobster dinner ($2.10), Ben Lombard a hamburger dinner ($1.42), and Clarence Dibert found a good pair of field glasses for $19. It came time for departure, but Bacon, Brodersen, and Ben L. put in a very belated appearance; result: each fined 35 cents and hot handed as the truck reeled down the road" at 7:40 p.m. "Hot handed" was not explained.

△ △ △

Via a slight detour near Hartford, Connecticut, we found *a new-mown hayfield, so everyone was soon trekking to a part of the field out of sight and shotgun range of the farmer's house a hundred yards from the truck. We carried plenty of canvas, for it was very damp; Bruce and Lloyd put up their mountain tent as usual.*

July 22. Monday, forty-one hundred miles from home, the journal continues, *Up at 6 a.m. in a heavy mist that drenched everything. We hastily packed the truck, hoping the farmer would not notice his trespassers. Cooking breakfast later at a roadside park, we were half thru [cocoa and mush] when thunder started a rain of cloudburst proportions. Hastily we finished and dashed for the protection of the canvas on the truck.*

Rain soaked, we drove into Hartford. It was there that we left Frank Brodersen, fourteen years of age, and after only ten miles out of town decided to push on to New Haven and Yale University. *It would be a good lesson to Frank to have to catch up with us in New York the best way he could,* Curtiss wrote.

While we all knew that any of us, if late enough, could be left behind, when it came time to actually drive on and leave a boy, we didn't seem to question it. A minority of the group did vote for returning to Hartford to look for him. Ten miles out of town didn't seem a big problem. But Frank would somehow be all right either way. We didn't know that Curtiss would soon make contact with the Brodersens in Oregon and with Boy Scout officers in New York, as well as putting a seven-state alarm out for Frank with their state patrol organizations. But at this point according to his journal, we simply drove on to New Haven and the famous university.

CHAPTER 10

New York and a Lost Adult

ON TO YALE University, then Danbury, Connecticut, and a cloudburst that had us using every bit of canvas we carried. Even so, rain splashed the sides and soaked the personal baggage in the blue boxes. A slide blocked the road to West Point, New York, requiring a long detour to cross the Hudson River. We arrived at The Military Academy more than an hour past when it closed its gate at five. We explained we had come clear across the country, so could an exception be made to the rule? Yes was the verdict.

The prestigious West Point institution perhaps piqued Curtiss's interest more than ours, given his Army WWI combat experiences. We had just visited major universities, perhaps to inspire us to continue our education after high school. But with the perspective of the American past to that time, the U.S. military had just completed the most popular war in our history, with few dissenters. The issues clear, the outcome proved conclusive with the unconditional defeat and surrender of first Hitler and then the Japanese emperor who had attacked Pearl Harbor and conquered Southeast Asia. We had yet to experience the Korean War, and the Vietnam conflict that inspired so much controversy. So a salute to the elite cadre of future officers seemed appropriate. We younger boys failed to understand the implications of the military draft that would soon face us at age eighteen.

After driving through the campus and later reaching the Scout Camp at Alpine, we found a large cabin that provided a welcome respite from the rain, with bunks, gas stove, even screens on windows and doors to keep out the mosquitoes. *By 12 midnight, all were in bed listening to the steady deluge outside— the drought in New England was over,* our Scoutmaster penned. It's wrong to underestimate the pleasure we felt at the luxury of being comfortable, warm, dry, and bugless. What relief in the driving rain! That night, in those luxurious bunkbeds of the crowded room, I clearly recall quartermaster Acton sitting up in bed in the middle of his sound sleep with a general announcement to all, *"That guy with the ragged ass is going to get his butt beat in."* With that, he laid back down to continue his sleep.

△ △ △

July 23. Despite rain and sleeping until nine, *with our best uniforms on, we jumped aboard the truck at 11 o'clock and huddled under canvas, singing our songs in the best of spirits.*

Our truck slithered and splashed seven miles to the great George Washington Bridge (toll 65 cents) across the Hudson (into New York City.) *As soon as Curtiss cashed some Am. Travelers checks, $5 was given to each boy. With this, most of the boys headed for the nearest automat. Bruce lost his wallet the first thing in the automat, but when it was turned in to the cashier, he loaded two trays with food before sitting down to a table,* Curtiss wrote with obvious amusement.

The small-town boys scattered to Rockefeller Center, the Music Hall, and the Rockettes, who bedazzled us. Empire State Building, Times Square—amazing. Yakima was never like that. All kinds of experiences packed into a couple of days that we have trouble remembering seven decades later. However, I do recall showing a cabbie in downtown Manhattan a silver dollar, common at home but rare on the East Coast. He shrugged, "Too bad it ain't American." Then I asked him which way would be north. He scratched his head, shaking it, and wrinkling his nose. "I know uptown, crosstown and downtown, but north?"

It was a happy bunch indeed that returned to the truck at 10:30 and told of their adventures for the 20-mile drive back to the Scout Camp, Curtiss penned. *Lyman had phoned the Manhattan Scout office, but no news of Brodersen did they have.*

July 24. Up at 7 a.m., off for the big city at 9:45 . . . pick up Ted Block at the George Washington Bridge and stopping at Grant's Tomb, where CRG had to threaten fines to keep Frank Bacon & Ben Lombard from climbing on the statuary.

Later, they and others in the group climbed up into the crown atop the Statue of Liberty. Dick Cole escaped to the museum and planetarium in Central Park, others back to Rockefeller Center, then the subway to Coney Island and Porter's favorite ride, the roller coaster. Curtiss continues the story, *There the fun began: the parachute jump, Ferris wheel, cyclone roller coaster, the steeple chase, gasoline and electric racing cars, as well as a regular restaurant meal. By 10 p.m., the boys were starting back to the big interurban station to take the subway back; Bruce and Lloyd did not arrive until 12:12, so received a fine of 90 cents each. At 1:20 a.m., we arrived at our sleeping quarters, so turned in with no foolishness.*

△ △ △

Our Scoutmaster does not explain his willingness to turn all of us loose to explore the big city on our own and find our way back by subway or other means. He seemed to have no doubt that we could pursue such adventures on our own and return safely. The chances of boys getting lost or not getting back to the rendezvous spot seemed high, but Curtiss, with apparent confidence in his Boy Scouts, indicated no worry. This time, it seems he didn't think of leaving us if we were late; instead he counted on levies of fines to keep us on time, one cent per minute.

Some might see the freedom Curtiss gave us to explore on our own as antithetical to our safety and security. He should have insisted on more rules and restrictions. But these come with fear and less trust.

Parents today may shelter children more than needed, restricting their freedom to explore and even fall at times. Curtiss clearly viewed learning from one's own mistakes or even misfortunes as important. Perhaps the best teachers in life. With trust in his Scouts' training, he could loosen the ties and allow more freedom, expecting his boys to act with responsible behavior. Somehow, we began to respond to that.

△ △ △

July 25. Fatigue started setting in when we hit New York. Our tireless leader wrote, *Although CRG and Lyman were up at 7:20, some of the boys had difficulty arising. We cleaned and swept the cabin. By the time the truck and icebox had been cleaned and the baggage loaded, it was 11:20 a.m.*

On the way to Philadelphia, *we tour the Delaware River Valley, looking for the Washington Crossing State Park. No drinking water, so we got back on the truck and ate lunch as we drove. Ben L. never could eat peanut butter, and we could not let him double on the tuna or lettuce sandwiches, so he waited patiently until the truck stopped.*

Coming into Philadelphia we bogged down in the traffic so that we could not get to Independence Hall before 5 p.m. However, we got to see the Liberty Bell and first meeting room of the U.S. Congress by looking thru the windows.

△ △ △

At York, Pennsylvania, we stopped beside a park till after dark, while we waited for Bob Petersen to return from visiting his uncle and aunt. It was getting late, and Curtiss, sitting up front in the cab, did not know that Lyman had gone to sleep on the grass. When Bob returned, we Scouts tiptoed back to the truck and climbed aboard, leaving our assistant Scoutmaster behind fast asleep as the truck quietly drove off. Sort of a joke, but with an edge since despite his contributions and humor, he seemed so different and not universally appreciated. Curtiss, oblivious that Lyman remained in York, describes the night's bivouac: *At 10 miles out, a hay field was spotted...a gate [was] opened, and soon the truck was disgorging the sleeping bags and sleepy boys...a beautiful night, for it was too cool for mosquitoes."*

July 28. We were nineteen days out and had travelled four thousand seven hundred miles. Curtiss wrote, *Up with the sun at 6:30. Fearing the farmer who owned the field might see us, we decided to push on and eat breakfast later. As we were rolling the last sleeping bags, someone asked, 'Where is Lyman?' Nobody knew. Since he had money, no one worried, for he could meet us in Washington, D.C. So at 7 o'clock, we pulled out toward Gettysburg.*

After taking in the famous battlefield area and breakfast, the troop continued on to Frederick, the home of Francis Scott Key and Barbara Frietchie. Though ads were spotted for Barbara Frietchie Candy, *we could find nothing of the good Old Lady's house, made famous by Whittier's poem.* Its most famous lines Curtiss knew: *"Shoot if you must, this old gray head; but spare your country's flag, she said."*

Curtiss's grasp of history and literature far exceeded ours. I don't remember studying the places and events as part of the trip or even appreciating the awful carnage of the Civil War at Gettysburg. Or Lincoln's historic address. We did benefit from the opportunities of engaging history and its sites and still remember some of them. But as kids, most of us didn't understand much of our heritage at the time.

As Curtiss didn't know why Lyman had disappeared, we weren't about to explain. The Boss didn't press the issue and seemed confident he would show up in Washington, D.C. So perhaps with a bit of internal guilt, we pressed on as usual.

CHAPTER 11

Washington, D.C.

DRIVING PAST THE White House in Washington, D.C., Curtiss recalled that, *we hurriedly dressed in uniforms and our best clothes and rushed to the Capitol. We didn't have the customary passes, but the Scout uniforms helped, so we were soon in the visitors' gallery of the House of Representatives. Representative Clare Booth Luce, one of the few women in Congress, was the best speaker. We moved on to the Senate, poor acoustics, climbed to the top of the Capitol dome, and then assembled at four-thirty near the truck.*

Curtiss's cryptic account doesn't describe the awe some of us felt at seeing the actual White House of our history and the current home of President Truman, its occupant since Roosevelt's death only two years earlier. Or at taking the elevator up to the gallery in the Congressional chambers to see our representatives debate in the Congress we had only read about. Without television, the only live images appeared in newsreels, shown in movie theaters usually before the featured film. But the speeches bored us, and we enjoyed running up the steps inside the Capitol dome to the highest level and looking far down at the rotunda below with its little people walking here and there.

△ △ △

But what about Frank? We had not found him in New York and wondered whether he had made it to Washington. I can still see a mental image of his return. We stood around the base of the Washington Monument, watching police cars race towards us, blue lights flashing and sirens shutting down. They stopped at the border of the grass surrounding the tower, and out jumped Frank and ran up to greet us. He laughed and regaled us with the story of his adventures in New York, including the Scout Executive's beautiful young daughter. It almost made me want to get lost.

The only problem—none of that story actually happened. My vivid memory over the years has romanticized Frank's return. I can still see it in my mind. Where do such memories come from? They take over from reality and block out the truth. They seem so real over many years and fixed in long-term memory until one becomes convinced that's what happened. That's why we needed Curtiss's writing of the saga to keep us straight before telling the story. So what did occur in Washington, D.C. to find the lost?

Turning to Curtiss's journal, we read, *A police car came along and asked if we had lost one of our number. When we said* we had lost two, they replied they had news of one, and would the one in charge come to the telephone to the City Police? We were informed that Frank Brodersen could be picked up at the apartment of Mrs. Rothe's friend. Mrs. Rothe was Scout Dick Rothe's mother.

While taking on more gas, Curtiss phoned Scout HQ to ask about Lyman. *He had not been heard from. We asked them to tell Lyman to come out to the Scout camp if he contacted the office.*

Curtiss describes the reality of the rendezvous with Frank, *So we drove thru Washington and up a fine street where many foreign embassies were housed. Stopped at last at the address of Mrs. Rothe's friend. Dick Rothe went in with Porter and returned with Frank, looking very clean and well. Dick then stayed with his mother's friend for the evening, while the truck went on to Silver Springs.*

Curtiss's brief note lacked much detail about Frank's story or his return. We must have had a celebration, but Curtiss' journal doesn't mention it, and few of us can remember what happened.

Five blocks north of Silver Springs, and Curtiss wrote, *who should they see walking along the road but their youngest adult leader? It seemed Lyman had spent the entire day after his arrival from York by train, sitting at the foot of the Washington Monument, thinking that would be one of the first places his comrades would visit. It would have been, had they not become so interested in the Capitol.*

So one boy we left behind for four days and three hundred miles, and our assistant Scoutmaster for almost two days.

One accidental, but we didn't return to get him, and the other intentional. What were their reactions on being separated or reunited? Lyman's we can surmise from subsequent later events. About Frank, more later.

Perhaps we had second thoughts, or possibly we just accepted what we did as "stuff happens." Maybe we took on our leader's stoicism to just move on and not worry about it.

He added, *At 10 o'clock, we drove out to the Reservoir Boy Scout camp, picking up Dick Rothe on the way.*

△ △ △

July 27. In his account, Curtiss relates, *Saturday, up at 7, but we could not get away until 9:45. At the Capitol "a policeman informed us that trucks are not allowed there but allowed us to get the pictures. Later, Ben Lombard and some of his kind tried to see Pres. Truman at the White House, but heard that the President was busy seeing his Sec. of State, James Byrnes, off to the airport to a meeting in Paris.*

Ben explains his recollections of the incident: *In regards to seeing President Truman, I thought there were just two of us, and it was based on a challenge from Bob Peterson. At the first guard station I asked the guard if we could have a meeting with the President. He said I needed to go to the second guard station. The guard at the second station said something about the Secretary of State, but we needed a pass to go further. I asked where I could get a pass, and he said from the White House. Then I asked, "How do I get a pass from the White House?" He said, "You don't!"*

I also asked if he had any brochures on the president, and that was the end of the conversation except the guard asked if we needed an escort off the premises.

Back in the Senate gallery, Curtiss wrote, *Sen. Mitchell from our state came into the gallery himself and explained who was speaking. After 1¼ hours Clarence and CRG nodded off to sleep a few times. Mr. Walsh of the Senator's staff took us to the Senate dining room for lunch. It was an ordinary meal in a very swell setting: mirrors, crystal chandeliers, negro waiters and a long table. We enjoyed meat stew and milk biscuits, topped off by the very best strawberry-pineapple-maraschino ice cream any of them had ever tasted . . . the lunch would be paid for by the Senator.*

Curtiss doesn't mention the actual cost from the menu: cup of soup, fifteen cents; apple pie, also fifteen cents; and on a French menu, the entire lunch with dessert, sixty cents.

United States Senate Restaurant

Saturday   July 27, 1946

LUNCHEON MENU

APPETIZERS

Clam Cocktail, 30
One-Half Grapefruit, 15

Fresh Crab-Meat Cocktail, 55
Celery and Olives, 35
Tomato and Clam Juice Cocktail, 20

Pineapple Juice, 15
Fruit Cup, 25

SOUPS

Senate Restaurant Bean, Cup, 10; Bowl, 15
Potage Mongole, Cup. 10; Bowl, 15
Jellied Beef Consomme, Cup, 15
Jellied Tomato Madrilene, Cup, 15

---

60 CENT LUNCHEON

Beef Saute Bourgeoise
Parsley Potatoes
Assorted Breads
Choice of: Chocolate Eclair or Ice Cream
Tea or Coffee

---

(1) **Hot Turkey Sandwich with Gravy**, Creamed Whipped Potatoes, Green Peas, 90
(2) **Cold Sliced Corned Beef**, Wisconsin Cheese, Potato Salad, Pickle, 85
(3) **Grilled Halibut Steak**, Parsley Potatoes, Sliced Cucumbers and Tomatoes, 85

DESSERTS

Apple Pie, 15
Fruit Jello, 15
Sliced Peaches, 35
Cup Custard, 15
Cupcakes, 10

Watermelon, 25
Chilled Cantaloupe, 20
Honeydew Melon, 25
Layer Cake, 15
Ice Cream, 15
Chocolate Eclair, 15

Coconut Custard Pie, 15
Bleu Cheese, 25
Gorgonzola Cheese, 25
Camembert Cheese, 25
Liederkranz Cheese, 25

BEVERAGES

Coffee, 5; Tea, 10
Coca-Cola, 10

Iced Coffee, 10

Golden Guernsey Milk or Buttermilk, 10
7-Up, 10

NO SUBSTITUTION ON THE ABOVE

△ △ △

At the Washington Monument the long lineup at the 10-cent elevator ride did not bother the boys. They went running, yelling, and yodeling all the way to the top. Some went up in 13 min.—notably Bacon; but for the climb, it took most of them 15–18 minutes.

Next ,the equally impressive memorials, to Jefferson and
to Lincoln. At the latter, Curtiss noticed the words engraved
on the granite walls beside "the seated emancipator's bronze
statue." Shortly before his assassination, concluding his second
inaugural address, our sixteenth president spoke from his heart:

> *Fondly do we hope—fervently do we pray—that this
> mighty scourge of war may speedily pass away. Yet, if
> God wills that it continue, until all the wealth piled by the
> bond-man's two hundred and fifty years of unrequited
> toil shall be sunk, and until every drop of blood drawn
> with the lash, shall be paid by another drawn with the
> sword, as was said three thousand years ago, so still it
> must be said "the judgments of the Lord, are true and
> righteous altogether."*
>
> *With malice toward none; with charity for all; with
> firmness in the right, as God gives us to see the right, let
> us strive on to finish the work we are in; to bind up the
> nation's wounds; to care for him who shall have borne
> the battle, and for his widow, and his orphan--to do all
> which may achieve and cherish a just and lasting peace,
> among ourselves, and with all nations.*

Profoundly moved today by Lincoln's wisdom and
perspective, I'm sure we skipped by it in 1946. George Bernard
Shaw remarked it is too bad that "youth is wasted on the young."
But we saw the memorials and have never forgotten them.

At the Pentagon the boys were stopped beyond the entrance

hall by the guards. At Robert E. Lee's mansion we were *"allowed to go thru...free of charge because we were a Scout party with a leader. Dick Rothe did a Jonah's whale stunt in the parking space and had to sit in the front seat a short time to recuperate."* Curtiss unfortunately doesn't explain the stunt. So much to see in Washington; *the evening program was do as you like until 11 p.m.*

△ △ △

July 28. Scoutmasters know food is important. *Acton and Mark [Gilbert] cooked mush, cocoa, and hot cakes. Ben L. as usual refused the bum breakfast, but at the first stop on the way to Annapolis, he was happy with potato chips, cupcakes, Pepsi Cola, and gum. After nearly losing Ben and Mark at a refreshment stand, the big blue truck rolled into the narrow streets of Annapolis.*

Dan McNamara especially enjoyed a visit to the Naval Academy.

The truck returned to Washington and the Congressional
Library, viewing the Declaration of Independence, Constitution
and Bill of Rights. Then off to General Washington's Mount
Vernon, where the neatly uniformed Scouts again did not have
to pay the small admission fee of 30 cents. Sometimes, it paid
to dress up. This time, we have an original description of who's
who in the picture, authoritative except for Curtiss's leaving out
Bob Comer, noted as 575, third from the left in the front row.

Troop 9 - Mt. Vernon - Geo. Washington's Home - July 46
From left - front row: Bruce Gilbert, Dick Cole,
     575, Frank Broderson, Frank Bacon, Ben Lombard,
     Don Bennett
2nd Row: Porter Lombard, Lloyd Johnson
3rd Row: Curtiss Gilbert, Dick Willard, Ken Sturgis,
     Ted Block, Dave Acton, Mark Gilbert,
     Bob Peterson, Dick Rothe, Clarence Dibert

As our experiences tallied up, Curtiss's descriptions of the some of the sites and our visits shortened until he just mentions the venue. Yet for others, like Williamsburg, he went into great detail. But the number and historical significance of all of them continues to strike us as the opportunities of a lifetime, which we appreciate mostly in retrospect. But they did pique interest in our past.

It was nearly 6 o'clock when the tired party headed down toward Richmond, Virginia. And at 7, a flat tire required another stop. A bent de-mountable rim. After an hour and a half delay, it was decided to drive to a big town on one tire of the dual. Everyone sat on the right side of the truck to save the tire. Ben L. had to be fined 50 cents before he understood the reason to keep his 150 lbs. over the good tires. Heading toward Williamsburg, at 11:20 a side road leading into a good growth of small pines beckoned the weary travelers to stop for the night. It was so cold, there were no mosquitoes.

CHAPTER 12

Cherokees, Gnats and Segregation

JULY 29. AGAIN, UP at seven, we reached Williamsburg, the restored city, two hours and one flat tire later. Curtiss continued, *A revolution here arose, led by Ken Sturgis, as to whether or not to stop here and see what the Rockefeller Foundation had worked so hard on. Those who followed Sturgis sat on the lawn; waiting for 2½ hours were Dick Allen, Dave Acton, Porter Lombard, Bob Comer and Dick Rothe, although Ben Lombard and Frank Bacon gave up their places toward the last of the tour so Rothe and Sturgis saw some of the colonial reconstruction. First, the Scouts paid 65 cents, got tickets to the 5 best exhibits. In the House of Burgesses their guide was a charming 18-year-old girl beautifully dressed in a light blue and white dress with hooped skirt.*

Much to be experienced of colonial times, but at 2:30 p.m., the group drove south.

△ △ △

Gilbert shared his impressions south of the Mason-Dixon Line. *Passing fields of cotton, corn, and tobacco with woods and swamps, a few dilapidated one- and two-story unpainted houses were occupied by Negroes, At one place on the road a cart carrying four cute little darky children and drawn by an old mule was passed. One-mule cultivators, followed by bowed figures, were noted working in the fields. At 6:30 a stop for supper at a neat little town named South Hill was made. When time to resume driving came, three boys had to be left behind—Sturgis, Cole and Brodersen.* Curtiss does not explain why they "had" to be left. Presumably for taking too much time. Frank must have thought, *Oh, no! Not again!* He had been buying a teddy bear for his sister while Sturgis and Cole played a pinball machine. Our Scoutmaster seemed relieved, however, possibly pleased for the first time about yet another tire problem. *Luckily for them, a flat tire forced a stop at a tire repair shop two miles down the road. They caught up there after hitchhiking . . . At 10:25 a stop for sleep was made in a field.*

△ △ △

July 30. Outside Raleigh, North Carolina, CRG continued his cryptic log. *Leave camp at 6:30 am after Bob Peterson carried out his threat to get the gang up more promptly. We found a place for breakfast, washed up, and ate our usual cocoa, mush, and cornflakes. Ted Block got in a scuffle with Bacon and loosened the braces on his teeth. By Peterson's energy, an hour was saved.* We're left wondering which was more important, saving an hour or Frank's teeth.

Passing rolling hills and signs telling of the Civil War, on the long grade to Ashville, a car came thumping along on a flat tire. They stopped and inquired for a car jack, so the boys helped them put on their spare tire.

Curtiss's account continues, *Hoping to reach the Smoky Mountains National Forest before dark, no stop was made at Asheville for supper. But hopes were soon lost because a 23-mile detour meant it was utter darkness when the Cherokee entrance to the National Forest was reached. The restaurant in the souvenir shop was open, so all were able to get a sandwich or two, served very neatly by good-looking Indian maidens. Several stocky, dusky Cherokee braves were proudly strutting around as though waiting for the waitresses to come off work. When Peterson and McNamara sort of walked by them close-like, challenging, it would not have taken much to start a fight.*

△ △ △

At a nearby public campground, he explained, *There were very few mosquitoes, but a new insect appeared. It bit sharply and was about four times more painful than a mosquito. They could pass four abreast through mosquito netting! The boys began to scratch within ten minutes after going to bed. Bruce and Lloyd got out a mountain tent, but the others thought a tent would be too warm, so slipped in the liners of their bags and slept poorly.*

That miserable night in the Great Smokies still stands out today to several Scouts. Brodersen writes today: *Hard to pick a most enjoyable place, probably Washington, D.C., as being back and part of the group was a relief. Worst is easy, the chiggers in the Smoky Mountains. Two or three of us bedded down. In the morning I was 10 feet down the slope from them and literally covered with small red dots.*

Dick Cole adds, *I vividly remember one night and morning in the Smoky Mountains. The warm temperature made it difficult to remain in one's sleeping bag. The mosquitoes, chiggers, were fierce. Early in the morning I said aloud "I just can't take it anymore." I was surprised when Curtiss said, "We might as well get moving."*

July 31. It was easy to get the bunch up for once. At 5:30 a.m., every one was dressing, Curtiss wrote. *Some washed clothes; other bathed in the shallow stream. Bruce and Lloyd had been free from gnats in their tent.*

Driving through the Great Smoky National Park, *the summit pass with its signs indicating trails reminded the party of the Cascade Crest Trail in Washington State. Matching pennies amused Acton, Sturgis, Johnson, and Cole. Peterson withdrew early in the game a heavy winner—15 cents. Through Chattanooga, new time zone, and up the contour ramp road of the National Park. At the entrance to the park, [the boys] paid an old gatekeeper 12 cents for over 16 years of age and 2 cents for under. The view over the edge was truly wonderful.*

The Tenn. R., Chattanooga, and all the rich farming country and wooded hills. At 2:45 p.m., most of the boys spent 10 cents going halfway down on the funicular railway.

Heading for Birmingham, Alabama, through a corner of Georgia, Curtiss commented, *Hardwood and pine sawmills and a barrel factory were passed. The logs on the logging trucks were very small, about 12" in diameter at the big end. Cotton and corn were doing fine. Pink myrtle, honeysuckle, blue sweet peas, and yellow daises were the principal flowers passed. Ben L. challenged Ted Block to a fight and got badly licked.*

△ △ △

Arrived in Birmingham 6:30. Negro quarter very poor. The streetcars were old-fashioned yellow ones divided, so the Negroes had to sit in a rear compartment. We had never seen this overt kind of segregation. Recall this was still the era of Jim Crow and before the bus boycotts and civil rights marches of the 1960s. Whites-only restaurants and restrooms confirmed the discrimination. It caused General Colin Powell to recall traveling to his first duty station in Alabama from his college in New York, "You had to have a strong bladder."

Curtiss noted a steel mill. *After eating at a cafeteria with the best and cheapest food yet. . . saw a great glow in the sky. So turned right, and a brightly lighted steel works belching fire was seen. Whenever a retort was emptied, the heated metal caused a fiery glow to light up the works. Leaving Birmingham behind, the party drove 50 miles before stopping at 10:30 in an old road.*

August 1. Curtiss explained in a note that morning, *As a damp fog settled and mosquitoes began to buzz too close, the Scoutmaster roused his sleeping charges at 5 o'clock, and at 5:30 the truck was underway. A heavy rain burst before the canvas had been put up. Bob Peterson, stripped to the waist, did most of the outside rope tying. The fumes from the exhaust were bad, and Dick Willard announced as he rushed to the rear, "I gotta puke." Canvas was put along the sides and around the rear, and it kept everyone busy plugging holes and keeping water from flooding seats and blue luggage boxes.*

△ △ △

Later at Gulfport, Louisiana, our travel-experienced Scoutmaster journaled, *We had lunch at a good cheap café, rolled along Lake Pontchartrain. The rain stopped and held off as we looked over the town of New Orleans.*

The French Quarter, the great Charity Hospital built by Huey Long, and the many shades of color in the skins of the populace—were all very interesting.

At 7:30 p.m., the truck plied the highway north to Baton Rouge, 82 miles of straight road covered in two hours through a swampy waste. Curtiss continued, *The capitol building was very high. Long was a great builder as well as a governor. A little dirty café was found open where the whole party could be fed. After waiting as much as 1½ hours for fried chicken to be cooked, during which time Ben L. broke the pinball machine and Frank B. finished demolishing another game of chance, the party put off again. Soon an oyster-shell surfaced crossroad was noticed running along a levee, so it was taken, and on the top of the levee behind a sign stopping traffic for construction ahead, the truck stopped for the night. Bedding rolls were laid out on the hard white oyster-shell road, so that no hip-holes could be dug; mosquitoes were plentiful, too.* So much for our leaders' laconic description of encounters in the Deep South. By now, we had become seasoned travelers and took most events in stride except for chiggers. Even breaking games of chance. He doesn't tell us which Frank did it.

CHAPTER 13

The Gulf, Portuguese Man-O-War, and Davy Crockett

AUGUST 2. "SWAMPY MISTS arose from the stagnant water near the levees," Curtiss observed. *Without stopping for breakfast, the boys hastened away at 5:30 and drove the 70 miles to Elton, where stopped beside a rice warehouse to clean up and make our own breakfast. Mark held up the departure for five minutes because he had felt the urge to wash his laundry, and now at this breakfast stop much more clothing was made ready for the drying clothesline on the truck.*

Into Texas, down to the Gulf Coast, we passed huge oil refineries. *Then on to the low sandy and shell-covered beach of the Gulf of Mexico. After repeated requests for a stop to go swimming, the truck turned off the highway and drove out to the beach, where it could serve as a dressing room.*

Led by Lyman, who had added his own observation as *the
instigator and loudest hollerer for a swim, getting OK from the
natives.* Curtiss continues his account, *The gang rushed for the
water and were soon 100 yds. off shore, jumping white-crested
waves and having a great time. Probably 15 minutes after
entering the water, Lloyd Johnson and Ben L. came back with
a most miserable expression on their faces. Lloyd was suffering
with an almost paralyzed arm and Ben from a numb hand—
both caused by touching a man-of-war jellyfish. Lloyd huddled
in the truck's cab for the rest of the day; Ben was not as hard hit.*

As we reveled in the warm water of the Gulf, the sand and
shallows extended far out. I recall wading and swimming toward
something blue floating in the water, like a small sail six inches
wide and only a few inches above the surface. The two of us raced
out to grab it. Instantly painful, the irritant seemed to cling to my
fingers. The pain crept up my arm, immobilizing it as we made
our way back to shore.

Ben remembers it vividly, *Just outside Galveston, Texas, we
stopped to swim in the Gulf. You could walk almost a mile in the
water from the beach. Lloyd Johnson and I spotted what looked
like a small, blue sail out in the water. We waded/swam out to
see what it was. Lloyd approached the sail first and reached out
to touch it. A Portuguese man-of-war, a large jellyfish with up to
30 ft. tentacles. Like grabbing a bolt of lightning. After touching
the jellyfish, Lloyd swung wildly, striking me in the chest, quickly
spreading the poisonous jolt. I made it to the shore, but Lloyd
needed help and had to be checked out at the Galveston Hospital.*

After the trip Ben was explaining the event to his mother and some of her church friends. *Lloyd and I were grabbed by a giant jellyfish with 30-foot long testicles.*

△ △ △

Other than Lyman losing his last pair of glasses and having another flat tire, requiring the purchase of a new one that cost $75.75, arriving in Houston proved unremarkable except for an inebriated Texan at a restaurant. Curtiss mentions, *He gave Lyman $5, wishing us "a fine time in Texas, the greatest state in the nation." We camped at a roadside park 70 miles out of Houston.*

Up at 5:30 a.m., August 3. We stopped at a roadside park at 8 for breakfast amid thorny trees among low rolling hills; everyone was hot and sticky. Had to put up the tarpaulin for shade.

Finally, San Antonio appeared, arising out of a desert of sagebrush. CRG drove thru town, trying to find the famous Alamo, where in the old Spanish Church plaques explained the main points in Davy Crockett's last stand there. Dick Cole and Ben Lombard jumped over a wall into a private garden and picked some green dates. They were fined 25 cents each. Bacon and Johnson also got into the forbidden garden and picked a number of green bananas, punishment a round of hacks, plus a 25-cent fine each. Punishment varied to fit the magnitude of the crime.

Our Scoutmaster continued, *Four hours of fuel pump trouble spoiled the afternoon. All that was needed was a new fuel pump, which was one of the spare parts carried under the seat. The 69 miles from San Antonio took all afternoon. Then there was another puncture that was fixed at Fredericksburg from 5:30 to 6:10. Bruce took over the black book [the boy's spending money accounts] from Sturgis. Supper was postponed until Brady was reached at 8:30—73 miles in 1 hour and 20 minutes. After the meal Frank Brodersen made a speech, presenting Don Bennett with a black brassiere, which some of the boys tried to put on Don.*

Looking back, Frank comments, *The brassiere presentation wasn't my idea, but I kind of recall being flattered because whoever initiated it thought I could speak. Don Bennett sticks in my mind as the kid who endured the most teasing.* He was a bit chunky, overweight.

Curtiss adds, *The Scoutmaster finally had to confiscate the garment.*

Boys could be a bit cruel to their young friend who did have a weight problem, expressed embarrassingly in his upper chest.

△ △ △

Navigator Bob Peterson by the lights of the service station consulted his road map and gave the cab, thru the intercommunication system, final directions concerning the roads to take to get to Carlsbad, so he could get an uninterrupted night's sleep. In Hobbs, Clarence hit a bump that broke two of the upper deck cross-poles and precipitated two of the Scouts into the lower deck, where they had to stay for 58 miles.

The three adults took turns driving and sleeping. For the

most part, we enjoyed a night's sleep while our generous leaders drove through the night to keep the schedule and to avoid traveling during the heat of the day.

CHAPTER 14

Heat or Mosquitoes? No Problem.
Drive All Night

AUGUST 4. AT 7:30 a.m., the beautiful town of Carlsbad, New Mexico, was reached; then we drove to the municipal river beach. While breakfast was prepared, the boys rushed for the blue waters of the lagoon. A long rope from a tree limb extending out over the water allowed big swings and dives. This and the fact that the boys could not be recalled from the water caused so late a departure for the caves that the 9:30 party was missed.

At 10:30 the troop, along with eight hundred others, entered the first big cave and the vaulted ceilings with stalactites of the most ghost-like shapes. Curtiss continued, *Descending, it became more intricate and complex until the climax of exquisite lace-like formations of the King's Chamber. After lunch it was either waiting in the long line for the 30-at-a-time elevator or walking up the long ramp we had descended. All the Scouts were willing to walk, and heading the line behind the neatly uniformed feminine guide, holding a steady pace, the 865 feet of elevation was made in 45 minutes.*

Ben recalls the repeated shouting as we ascended—to hear the echoes bouncing off the rock walls of the caverns at different levels. The echoing sounds sometimes reflected the smirks of their originators. The choice of words did not always jibe with the Boy Scout oath.

Not having acquired a love for spelunking, I nevertheless enjoyed the caves of the Carlsbad Caverns with their spectacular stalagmites and stalactites. They live vividly in the mind's eye to this day, although I have never revisited the caverns.

△ △ △

As we were leaving for Roswell in the early evening, Curtiss reported, *A terrific explosion that nearly blew a board off the floor of the truck indicated another of our tires had blown out, After putting on the spare tire, having supper in Roswell, and putting up the bunks, with the boys in their sleeping bags, about 11 o'clock we realized gas had been forgotten at Roswell, and the tanks were nearly empty. A nearby Phillips petroleum station turned out its lights just as the truck pulled in, but the tanks were again filled. Thus, when Curtiss, Block, and Clarence stopped for the night at 12:30 and rolled out their bedrolls beside a range fence just off the road, their minds were at ease.*

August 5. After five hours' sleep, the trio climbed back into the cab and without waking the boys resumed the journey. The intense heat in Las Vegas, New Mexico, explained the houses of foot-thick adobe. The day driving through the dry New Mexico countryside led to Black Mountain Boy Scout camp in Philmont, where Curtiss enjoyed *the best campfire any of us had ever seen. Our part was a little skit on how we acted while sightseeing in a big city and a recital of the itinerary.*   ·

August 6. With one month of travel behind them, the Scouts headed north in New Mexico to Taos. The boys sang and practiced songs they had heard at the campfire the night before. Brodersen finally found a place where he could parcel post his $5 bear as a present to his sister. While en route to Santa Fe, lunch was served and another excellent potato salad mixed up by David Acton.

Through picturesque Santa Fe, then Albuquerque, the determined leaders drove into the night. A sudden rainstorm drenched the boys on the top deck until they wired down the protecting canvas tarp.

All went well until just after midnight, when another flat tire forced a two-hour halt for a jerry-rigged repair placing new boots in the tire casing. The repairs held out for just three hours before the tire went boom again. Two blowouts by 5:30 in the morning. We limped into Winslow to spend the last traveler checks to make the $85 transaction for a new tire. By this time we'd lost count of the number of tire blowouts.

△ △ △

August 7. By 6:30 the group was on the way to Flagstaff,
Arizona, toward the entrance to the Grand Canyon National
Park. There, an Indian guide was hired to tell of the canyon
and the efforts of the Indians in securing rain. After lunch and
a little football despite the heat, the truck took the party to
many other panorama points. The curio shops took more of
the boys' time than did the scenic grandeur, Curtiss observed.
Possibly because of the shops' air conditioning. We'd become
hot and tired and perhaps overloaded with the grandeur and
spectacular scenes we had seen.

After the day spent at the Grand Canyon, another night
drive began. As we approached the state border, Clarence, who
had been driving, and Lyman woke up CRG, who had taken a
3-hour nap in the back of the truck, and let him drive through
the Arizona inspection station, where they were much put
out because copies of insurance policies protecting the lives
of the boys were not carried in the truck. After getting a good
lecture on careful driving, we ware allowed to proceed into
the early morning hours. Many of us didn't know we each had
life insurance.

August 8. We stopped at a desert flat spot while several
Scouts and Curtiss piled out and unrolled their sleeping bags
among the yucca plants. *At 6:30 the sun was up and hot enough*
to make it uncomfortable except when traveling. After touring
Boulder Dam and having breakfast under a willow tree, Dan
McNamara and Dick Cole had haircuts, but most of the boys

thought $1 too high. The rest of the day, the boys enjoyed the robin-egg blue warm waters of the huge reservoir, Lake Mead, spanning the border of Arizona and Nevada.

△ △ △

Refreshed from the swim, Curtiss wrote, *The group roared down the 20 miles to Las Vegas, Nevada. The glitzy city, lighted up at night, looked like a page torn from a cheap magazine. Anyone could see all the gambling devices and people playing them. It really gave the boys an eyeful.*

He let us wander the streets on our own after finding cheap restaurants for dinner. He must have known minors were excluded from the casinos.

At 9 p.m. with the truck made up for night driving, the boys watched the bright lights of Las Vegas disappear as Clarence and Curtiss piloted them from the wicked city. Out onto the desert, the heat was not noticeable as long as the truck was making its own 40-mile-an-hour breeze.

CHAPTER 15

California Communication

August 9. Day and night must have seemed mixed up with all-night driving, but, Curtiss wrote, *We were up at 5:10 and continued on busy Highway #66 without waking the boys. . . came into the San Bernardino Mts. And lost elevation from 5000 ft. to 2000 ft. The boys put on their best clothes they had left and argued about what they would do in Los Angeles. Since money was short, CRG promised to cash a check at his apple broker's office.*

Curtiss explained the plan, *Porter, Ben, and Brodersen were to go to Long Beach to see the Lombards' uncle, Ted Block to see an aunt and uncle, while the rest planned to stay with the truck. All would meet at a rather hazy point in Santa Monica at 5 p.m.*

The group toured several places, finally to the fruit and cold storage and office of Hall-Haas and Vessey, longtime marketers

for Gilbert Orchards. Not only did Mr. Vessey cash the personal
check of $250, but he made a $25 present to the troop for a treat.
When everyone got on the truck, they found a box of peaches
and ripe pears, which the Vesseys had given them.

After visiting the Rose Bowl and Hollywood, the troop was
passing Beverly Hills residential district on the way to Santa
Monica when Ted Block and his uncle's family came along
in their car. Dave Acton and Dan McNamara arrive [at the
meeting point] on time, but the Lombard party fails to show
up. Frank Bacon took a short swim, Lyman Bailey saw Errol
Flynn's sea-going yacht, and others toured the pier and beach
until 6, when it was decided to start north without the missing
3. The drive up the excellent highway was beautiful.

At 7:20 the siren of a red-spotlighted police car came up
from the rear and motioned for the truck to pull up alongside the
road. Two cops jumped out and announced the missing three
were coming with their relatives from Los Angeles, and the truck
should stay where it was. But when no one came for a half hour,
Curtiss decided to push on so the boys could be getting something
to eat at one of the numerous roadside hamburger stands. But
after the meal and after the bunks had been put up, still there was
no Porter and his party, so at 9:25 the journey continued.

Getting left behind became old hat to Brodersen, this his
third time. For Porter, the second. Curtiss didn't seem to worry
about them—or police instructions. His concern: the rest of the
boys in the truck, first hungry and then sleepy. Porter would
take care of the situation and the younger boys. Indeed, the

three did the wise thing. They contacted the police to find the missing truck.

Our intrepid leader, following his pattern of not deviating significantly from the schedule, again drove us on, knowing that the Lombards and Brodersen would find a way to catch us. *At Oxnard the cops again stopped the truck and said the missing 3 could be located thru the police station at Santa Barbara. At 10:30 from a Standard service station Curtiss got word from the police station to call the Lombards' grandmother, and in 15 minutes Mr. and Mrs. Calhoun with the missing 3 rejoined the party. Since the truck was parked directly beneath streetlights, the Calhouns climbed up to where they could see the weary Scouts, all sound asleep in their sleeping bags. The reason Porter's party had missed the truck was because there had been a misunderstanding about where in Santa Monica the rendezvous was to be.*

△ △ △

August 10, CRG recognized fatigue. *Got under way without awakening the boys. At San Louis Obispo and a breakfast pullover, Ted Block stopped with Bob Peterson to phone home. He was not feeling too well and talked only of home. Lyman ate his own jam; he was getting tired of cold cereal, too.*

Toward the end of the trip, the Scout who earlier endured the brassiere incident mispronounced San Jose. Laughing, we made him shout "San Joes " all the way through town. Not nice.

In Palo Alto at Stanford University several of the older boys were conversing with Yakima High's drama instructor Miss

Burke. She stayed on the truck as far as the interurban station. Sophisticated lady, but willing to get on the truck with a bunch of scruffy Boy Scouts and ride for a ways. She personified drama and the arts in her attractive appearance as well as speech.

Scouts at Stanford University

△ △ △

Clarence took the truckload of Scouts into the western section of San Francisco. Curtiss shared, *A stop was made at a Safeway grocery store; Lyman was left behind at this stop and not missed until noses were counted in order to pay the toll bridge fare at the Golden Gate Bridge. In the fog and cold, the truck returned back across the bridge to San Francisco, experiencing the usual kidding of the outlandish van and party by the guards as the truck passed through the tollgates. The boys found a cheap restaurant on Fisherman's Wharf for dinner at $1.25.*

Returning to the truck, everyone had one guess as to where Lyman might be found—the police station. So Curtiss phoned, and sure enough, Lyman was there in the missing persons department. A. little later, Lyman hailed the truck from the steps of the police station.

Deprived of his notes, we don't know what happened or how the young schoolteacher felt at being left once again.

The truck threaded thru streetcars, taxis, and expensive limousines in the Saturday 9 p.m. traffic, looking for a place to sleep. Finally, high on Market Street in a vacant lot, an open space perhaps 150 ft. square was spied in the driving fog. Bunks were made up on the truck for all except Clarence and Curtiss, because the ground was hard-baked clay. The top canvas was spread over the truck because the fog was very damp and cold. All slept well, even the two on the ground.

Creative camping. Hard to visualize the big truck in a small vacant lot in the middle of busy San Francisco with the cold fog rolling in off the Pacific and through the Golden Gate.

August 11. In the cold wind and fog blowing hard, they all stayed in bed until 8:30. Since the thick fog had blotted out much of San Francisco the afternoon before, it was decided to spend a few hours driving about town before breakfast. Ben Lombard, in trying to make one of his late climbs onto the truck as it started, stumbled on a curb, fell, struck his head on the concrete, and was pulled almost from under the wheel by Bob Comer.

Ben recalls, *Early that morning, the signal was given that the truck was leaving. As usual, everybody waited until the truck was doing about 30 miles an hour* [probably five] *before racing, running, and diving for the truck's sideboards. Bodies were flying everywhere, and all made it except Ben, who missed the truck and dove into the street curb. Ben had a bump the size of a goose egg, but survived with a slight concussion. He earned the coveted ride in the cab for the whole time in San Francisco.*

In Curtiss's version, *Dazed and sick, Ben was put in the front seat with the truck driver, where he soon recovered from what he termed his ailment, magnesia.*

△ △ △

Later that day at Yosemite National Park, Curtiss describes the beauty of the valley's great granite walls, and the waterfalls, diminished well after the spring snowmelt. At 10 p.m. after the dramatic bonfire hurtling down Half Dome's precipice, we drove back to the campground for a good night's sleep. Curtiss notes that it was easy to find Yosemite's Camp Curry, the old camping place the party had had in 1941, during an earlier truck excursion to California.

CHAPTER 16

Heading Home

August 12. Traveling up the California interior valley, without much to interest either Curtiss in the cab or the boys in the back, we had to find something exciting to do. Old Highway 99 provided just two lanes. So when a soda-pop truck loaded with drinks pulls up behind us to pass, several Scouts scramble up the side rack. The mother lode of all soft drinks slowly passes—only four feet away. At fifty-plus miles an hour. Temptation overwhelms good judgment. Never mind the streaking pavement below. The participants all reach out over the four-foot gap, trying to maintain balance, hanging on to the top slat for dear life. Feet braced on a lower one. Easy does it. Just a little more lean and stretch. Quick, the truck's passing. A shout goes up. One of the smaller guys holds up a full bottle of pop.

How Dick Cole did it without a catastrophe, he never explained.

It did provide some relief for the boredom until the troop arrived after midnight to camp on a school grounds at the foot of Mount Shasta.

August 13. The boys were awakened so that they could see the mountain, elevation 14,140 feet. It was unusually bare of snow, but looked like a big day's work for one who would try to climb it.

Curtiss enjoyed every mountain vista perhaps more than we did at such an early hour. But by this time, since we'd had much more sleep than our leaders, it didn't seem to bother us.

△ △ △

The truck pushed on and crossed into Oregon two hours later. *At Crater Lake National Park, on the crater rim, the boys got their first glimpse of the deep blue waters filling the old crater of Mount Montezuma. From a big snowbank, our ice box was filled with snow; here also, Dave Acton received a hard snowball in the eye from Bob Peterson's pitching arm. So David had to sit in the cab for most of the day.* The snow in August reflected the high elevation of the crater rim enclosing the deep blue lake.

Curtiss continued, *At the observation point the boys climbed to a fire lookout station on a little peak called the 'Watchtower.' Porter, Sturgis, Rothe, Bacon, Cole, Willard, Allen, Dan, Bruce, Lloyd, and Ben registered at the summit. Lyman Bailey turned back just short of the top because he thought the others had turned back and he might be left behind again. While waiting, he lay down on the warm pumice and fell asleep. Fifteen minutes later, the others returned and, thinking it would be a good joke, jumped on the truck and left poor Lyman snoring comfortably. It was only two miles around to the cafeteria and hotel, and soon after everyone had washed up and were preparing lunch in the back of the truck, here came Lyman, looking black as a thundercloud. It was hard to make him believe it was all a joke.*

The three leaders and seven of the boys took the trail two thousand feet down to the boat landing on the lake, where many took rowboats for a trip on the purple water. Bruce and Lloyd rowed a mile to Wizard Island. This made them 15 min. late for the 5 o'clock departure, so they had to pay a 15-cent fine each.

△ △ △

In Bend, Oregon, it was 50 degrees cold. Curtiss made a phone call to Yakima, announcing the return of the Scouts about 10 the next morning. *After a steak restaurant dinner from Los Angeles treat money, the truck rolled north over the waste and range country of northern Oregon. At 2 a.m., among the rolling hills covered with wheat fields, turned off on a dirt road so that Clarence and CRG could roll out their sleeping bags for 3½ hours of sleep.*

August 14. At 6 a.m. with the boys still in their bunks, awakened enough to see the snowcapped peaks of several volcanic mountains: Jefferson and Hood in Oregon, Adams, Rainier, and St. Helens in Washington. Recall the beautiful symmetrical pyramid of St. Helens before she blew her top off later on in 1980.

Curtiss added, *The truck continued toward the Columbia R. 20 miles away. The ferry, consisting of a sturdy little tugboat lashed to a barge, was coming across to welcome the happy travelers. After paying $1.50, the ten-minute crossing was made, and the dry shores of the state of Washington received its young citizens once again.*

He continued. *No restaurant was open in Goldendale at 7:20, and besides, the boys were still in their bags, so it was decided to hurry on. A stop was made on Satus Creek so the bunks could be rolled up and everyone given a chance to wash. It seemed like a dream to be passing thru Toppenish, Buena, and Union Gap and to realize the 1000 adventures we had experienced were to be climaxed by a safe return to the city limits of Yakima. The junky views along south First and the rough pavement of Yakima Ave. were soon passed, and at 10:40 a.m., the happy travelers were back in Curtiss's yard, from whence they had started 39 days before. A newspaper photographer had his inning before everyone scattered to his home to be welcomed by much-relieved parents.*

Speedometer reading 74372 – total 10,706 miles.

△ △ △

Our Scoutmaster ended his journal in a triumphant mood. We arrived safely home, on time, to happy parents and interested newspaper reporters. Yakima seemed smaller than when we left, but we looked forward to a soft bed and Mom's cooking. We also knew the full story remained to be told.

Yakima Boy Scouts Back From 10,000-Mile Tour

Boy Scouts and adult leaders of Troop No. 9 returned to Yakima yesterday after a 10,000-mile cross-country tour by truck.

Shown above in upper row, left to right, are Kenneth Sturgis, Ben Lombard, Frank Bacon, Dick Cole, Dick Allen, Don Bennett, Bob Comer and Dick Rothe.

In the center row, left to right are Mark Gilbert, Clarence Dilbert, driver, Bob Peterson, Dan McNamara, Dick Willard, David Acton and Ted Block.

In the bottom row, left to right, are Lyman Bailey, assistant scoutmaster, Frank Brodersen, Bruce Gilbert, Lloyd Johnson, Porter Lombard and Curtiss Gilbert, scoutmaster. (Republic)

CHAPTER 17

What Really Happened after Hartford

FRANK BRODERSEN, THE fourteen-year-old boy left behind in Hartford, three thousand miles from home, with two cents in his pocket, didn't catch up to us for four days and over three hundred miles. How did he manage?

Our recollections are hazy, sometimes romanticized, or as mine, flat-out wrong. The seven-state alarm put out for Frank added excitement. Why we didn't connect in New York remains a mystery. One theory: two Scout offices contacted separately, city and national, and they didn't communicate.

Recollections can grow with the telling. The reality may be less romantic, even grim, but filled with the resilience of youth. So here is what really happened, in Frank's own memory and words. They have the ring of truth:

On July 22, 1946, a wet morning started the day of my most vivid memory. Later that morning, when the Hartford Post Office stop was made, I decided to send a couple of postcards home. Another Scout was also in the little basement area where a standup desk provided a writing surface. He finished and left; Porter poked his head in before quickly leaving. Shortly thereafter, I had a funny feeling, but hadn't heard any shouting and was confident someone would alert me to any imminent departure. To this day, I remember the sinking feeling in my stomach when I went outside and found no big blue truck.

I was really scared. Because we were going to be at Coney Island in just a few days, I had not drawn any money from my spending account. There were literally two pennies in my pocket. Wearing dirty corduroy pants and an old jacket, needing a bath and clean clothes, I was also pretty scruffy. In a nearby small service station, I used a bathroom and asked how to get to West Point, which was the next stop I remembered. The answer was to use the new freeway or take the older highway. Having no experience with a four-lane "freeway," it seemed far less scary to try hitchhiking on smaller roads.

The morning clouds had mostly dissipated when I started walking, and other than one youngster in the yard of a country home who asked who I was, no one spoke, no one stopped, and I just continued walking, trying to get a ride from every passing car. When one car stopped, I ran to reach it, but they were just looking at a map and ignored me, driving off. I had no plan beyond trying to get to West Point. There wasn't a great deal of traffic. Was I even on the right road? It was continually depressing when no one slows down or gives you a second glance.

Late in the afternoon, about 13 miles from Hartford, a guy in a new Chevy coupe stopped and asked me where I was headed. When I explained about the Scout trip, missing the departure, and where I hoped to go, he wasn't too sure I was being truthful. He said he'd been stationed in Oregon north of Corvallis. I asked, Camp Adair? He said, you must be from Oregon; no one else has ever heard of Camp Adair. He said he was a liquor or beer salesman.

I have no memory of the highway numbers or names of the roads I used. West Point is roughly due west of Hartford; the Scouts went south to New Haven first and then NW to West Point, a "V" shaped route. The guy who picked me up took me to the police station in Danbury, Connecticut. It seemed to take a quite a long time after the officer in charge interviewed me before they decided to take me to a bed and breakfast. I don't know whether or not my parents were called or who paid for the overnight stay. I just did as I was told.

The B & B was super clean, had a "fluffy" décor, and was delightfully comfortable. The owner was an older woman who graciously fed me breakfast. Another officer picked me up, and later they staked me with $20 and put me on a bus from Danbury to New York City. I was instructed to stand at a specific location where a Scout employee met me. He confirmed my identity and took me to the Scout office. That evening, a Scout executive took me to his home in New Rochelle, New York.

He had a daughter about my age. After dinner, he took my filthy clothes and underwear to be washed. I was really embarrassed. Based on my vague memory of the tone of a dinner table conversation, my guess is the Scout executive's wife wasn't real happy with a 14-year-old ragamuffin in her home. It continued for three days, and after the first one her daughter disappeared. We'd had fun, visiting and I think walking downtown the first day. But she was "busy" after that.

One night at dinner, the Scout executive's wife asked if he'd checked at a specific Scout campground. He responded in an irritated fashion that it was closed. I'm pretty sure that was where the gang had camped. I spent one day just sitting and another in New York City, mostly at the Scout office— but they did arrange for me to see the Rockettes. I asked why they couldn't find the big blue truck. Did they check the Battery and Coney

Island? The Scout exec said the police had been notified and were looking. It was frustrating. Viewed from the standpoint of today's common communications, it's amazing that we didn't reconnect in New York City.

Eventually, enough "long distance" calls were made, and on July 26th I was given a ticket to Washington, D.C., and taken to Grand Central Station. In Washington, I was to meet a relative or friend of another Scout. How this was set up was never explained, but my guess is my folks and other parents made the arrangements. At Union Station, when no one appeared to be looking for me, I sat in the waiting room for a long, long time. Finally, a woman tapped me on the shoulder and asked, "Are you...?" and took me to her apartment. (She'd expected to see a boy in a Scout uniform.) After we arrived at her upscale home, the time went by slowly, but eventually the doorbell rang, Scouts appeared, and my adventure was over.

△ △ △

These heart-warming stories tell of the kindness of those who helped us along the way. We can be forever grateful to God for his protection and to the friends and parents who meant much to us so long ago— even if they are no longer around to receive our thanks.

EPILOGUE

HOW DO YOU put this true story in perspective in 2016, 70 years after the trip, when the boys have themselves become old . . . those still alive? It could never happen today for many reasons and seemed improbable even then. The account would never have surfaced again after sleeping for 67 years except for Cragg Gilbert's finding his grandfather's journal.

Our beloved Scoutmaster died only fourteen months after the trip at age fifty-three. Much too early. With so little sleep, and so much stress of responsibility for a sometimes-wild bunch of kids, we have to wonder whether the trip contributed to his early demise.

You may not agree with his decisions. He had a schedule to meet, and many parents counted on it. Curtiss practiced Admiral Farragut's order in 1812: "Damn the torpedoes, full speed ahead." Perhaps he believed that his Scout training produced boys resilient enough to cope with adversity and learn from it. He could leave his young men to find their way back if necessary. And with help along the way, they always returned.

But he did what was in his heart to do for all of us and for all his appreciative Scouts before us, over twenty-six years of selfless giving of time, effort, resources, and wisdom. He conceived the ideas, planned the adventures, and carried them out successfully.

△ △ △

Were the risks Curtiss Gilbert embraced wise? Did he take undue chances at that time? One era's character-building work may be another's negligence. Times change. Parents then as now looked to teachers and youth leaders to inspire and develop character in their kids. It's just done differently now.

Curtiss's granddaughter Betsy Mann alleges that we may now hover too much over our children, depriving them of learning by their own decisions and mistakes, the "helicopter parent." Or the "snowplow" ones who want to remove every training hurdle out of the way so the child never learns to deal with the obstacles in life.

On the other hand, we now cheer on our young football and soccer players who risk serious head injury and even death with concussions. Seemingly, in American football, the harder they collide, the better. Or we encourage them in Iron Man and Marathon contests, which reach the limits of physical endurance and risk.

We can judge the past by our current ideas of leading children. Or should we? Which are better or worse? How do you balance risk versus benefit? What risks are worth taking?

In the larger view, how did Curtiss's faith impact what he did for boys over so many years? Did God honor whatever faith and trust he possessed? Did he pray for his Scouts? He taught boys in Sunday school at his church. Though quiet about his faith, perhaps we can understand it best by what he did. And the tributes lavished upon him by so many speak to us about what lived inside the man. Like the Biblical principle: "I will show you my faith by what I do."

△ △ △

But what of the boys in the truck? What has happened to them, or rather who have they become? What have they done with their lives? How did the adventures with Curtiss Gilbert affect their choices over the years? Did he succeed in helping our parents make boys into men—those who would contribute to make their part of the world a better place?

It seems only the younger Boy Scouts on the trip have lived to tell of the adventures. All seven of us now approach our mid-eighties.

You have followed several of the older boys in the story: Bob Peterson, our navigator with the knee infection left in a Minneapolis hospital; Ted Block with the booming voice, our senior patrol leader and boss who took his job seriously; the untiring quartermaster, cook, and organizer, David Acton. Mark Gilbert, Bruce's unselfish middle brother, died in his early fifties just like his father, Curtiss, probably from heart disease. All of the other former Scouts on the trip we want to honor as well, some possibly deceased, who shared the adventure with us. We. have not found: Dick Allen, Don Bennett, Bob Comer, Dan McNamara, Dick Rothe, Ken Sturgis, and Dick Willard.

△ △ △

But the surviving seven enjoyed a reunion in Yakima in September, 2014 that brought us together, some for the first time in sixty-eight years. Sharing stories, we learned of each others' families and lives.

The survivors at Gilbert Orchards, 2014, no truck in sight.
From left, Lloyd Johnson, Ben Lombard, Frank Brodersen,
Bruce Gilbert, Porter Lombard, Frank Bacon, Dick Cole

We all, subject to the military draft, spent at least two years in the military service either during the Korean War in 1950–52 or, with an academic deferment, afterwards. All seven married and lived adventurous lives, whether mountain climbing, helicopter skiing, working with kids through Scouts, Young Life or their churches. Some have served on various boards, established successful businesses, practiced surgery or law, traveled and worked internationally, became professors at universities, and authored books. Most still have good health and continue to pursue active lives.

△ △ △

Frank Brodersen writes, "After being left in Hartford, I think I had to catch up three times. It never bothered me. Today I wonder why I never had the sense to carry money."

After the trip, Frank returned to his home in Forest Grove, Oregon, where he graduated from Pacific University. He served in the military and has been married to Jil for 57 years. A businessman, Frank also served in leadership of Rotary and other community and professional organizations. He and Jil now live in Virginia near their children and grandchildren.

△ △ △

Dick Cole became an integral part of the adventure, an Eagle Scout, prominent athlete in high school skiing and baseball. He lettered in baseball at Stanford, and after college and the Army, graduated from law school there and practiced law in Fairbanks, Alaska for over thirty years. Dick still flies his own airplane to the interior, a resident of Anchorage, Alaska. He and Barbara, his wife since 1958, also spend part of their year in Seattle.

△ △ △

Ben Lombard grew up in Yakima, hiking, climbing mountains, graduating from Yakima High School. After serving in the Navy for four years during the Korean War and beyond, he graduated from the University of Washington in 1958. Skiing also became important and remains so to this day. He still maintains his real estate business in Yakima. Active in Scouting, he continues to live out his admiration for Curtiss Gilbert; the effect his old Scoutmaster has had in many young men's lives has stayed with him. Ben, still known for his sense of humor, is married to Linda Lee in Yakima. They have two daughters, both in Yakima, and one granddaughter. They remain enthusiastic in telling the story of the big trip.

△ △ △

Porter Lombard joined Troop 9 in 1942, which encouraged him to experience mountain climbing and hiking. He graduated from Pomona College and earned his PhD at Washington State University and later at Michigan State University in Horticulture. After serving two years in the Korean War, he served as a citrus researcher in California and subsequently moved to Oregon. He introduced wine grapes crops in western Oregon starting in 1967 through his faculty position at Oregon State University. He married Corinne in 1974, and both continue to climb and hike. Their favorite climb is Mount Shasta. Early on, Porter worked with youth groups for climbing and hiking through the 1960s and '70s. It surprised him how well the teenage girls did on their hikes. Retired now, Porter and Corinne live in Medford, Oregon.

Curtis Gilbert contributed Bible and war stories of WWI for a young Porter. Before our big trip, recall that Curtis led Porter and others on an excursion to the Snake River and a climb of the Oregon Matterhorn. While Porter couldn't summit the peak, it inspired his own climb of the Swiss Matterhorn twenty-six years later.

△ △ △

Frank Bacon joined Troop 9 at age thirteen, the year he met Suzanne, his future wife. Curtiss inspired his Scouting experience, becoming a Life Scout, his love of creation, and his lifelong values. Graduating from the University of Washington in business administration and ROTC, he served in the U.S. Air Force from 1955 to '58 and later developed thriving businesses in Yakima.

His lifelong devotion to young people, Scouting, coaching, and church youth leadership has led to community involvement, significant awards, board assignments, and mission projects, particularly in Ethiopia. Active in Scouting, Young Life, and their own church, Frank and Suzanne still live in Yakima, enjoying their two children's families, eight grandchildren and two great-grandsons.

△ △ △

Bruce Gilbert continued his interest in mountain climbing, graduating from Washington State College, now University. He served two years in the Peace Corps in Sierra Leone, Africa. Only 16 at his father's death, he later declined to join his brothers

Cragg and Mark in Gilbert Orchards growing fruit. He married Gail Mitchell and settled in Haines, Alaska, where he developed a multifaceted business in outdoor goods and hardware. His expeditions have included a climb in 1958 of Denali, elevation over 20,300 feet, at that time named Mount McKinley. He and Gail have two children, a daughter in Haines helping with the business, and Scott, a successful businessman in Seattle.

△ △ △

Three of Curtiss's grandchildren—Cragg Gilbert, Jr., now running Gilbert Orchards in Yakima; Betsy Mann, a parent educator in Ottawa, Ontario; and Scott Gilbert, Bruce's son in Seattle—could not have been more helpful and supportive in so many ways in telling the story of the Big Trip and their outstanding grandfather.

△ △ △

My story as author/editor is published on the back cover of this book. It doesn't mention a lifetime of leaning into adventure inspired by our Scoutmaster. This includes climbing all the high volcanic peaks in Washington, working as a Seattle-based surgeon/teacher here and at a University in Ethiopia for three years. I also volunteered for short periods in mission hospitals in India, Pakistan, and Kenya. It does include the audacity of now trying to tell the story in America of our friends in Bethlehem by using fiction, recently publishing *Living Stones, Cry of Hope and now Uprooting the Olive Tree*. We lived there on two occasions, learning of friends' suffering under 48 years of military occupation.

I live with my wife Marianne in Edmonds, Washington; most of our children and grandchildren also live in the Seattle area.

△ △ △

Finally, sharing this improbable narrative with comrades in Scouting from 70 years ago, and now with others, brings all of us a great deal of pleasure.

ACKNOWLEDGEMENTS

TO CRAGG GILBERT, Jr., who unearthed his grandfather's journal among the dusty archives of the past, we owe the opportunity to tell this story of men and boys over two generations ago. Cragg assisted us in providing additional information, and his support proved invaluable.

Betsy Mann, daughter of Curtiss's oldest child Marion, spent days editing the manuscript, adding information and correcting my errors. Thanks to John Baule, director of the Yakima Valley Museum, her diligent search in Yakima and scanning of records and pictures enabled telling the story better than thousands of more words. Her guidance is itself a significant contribution to the annals of the Gilbert family.

Frank Bacon took Curtiss's notes, printed them into "The Big Trip," and sent it to us surviving scouts, enabling the story to be told. He organized and led us along with Ben Lombard, both of Yakima, in getting together. Their enthusiasm, support, contributions, and leadership drove the project forward.

The original story, *Where's Frank*, shorter, written for the participants and our families, generated interest in others as well, including Scout leaders, Walter Mueller, executive, as well as Bruce Heiser and Robert Sinclair. These men lent their support to enlarge the readership through publication and tell the account of Troop Nine's unusual adventure of long ago.

All of the seven surviving scouts have renewed our friendship after so many years, and all have contributed in many ways to put the trip into focus through their eyes and recollections. Their vigorous expressions of support and that of their families have pushed this through to an enlarged story with human interest beyond the facts of a travelogue, including a tribute to our Scoutmaster.

John Koehler, publisher, and Joe Coccaro, executive editor, made the story into a book, catching the spirit of adventure and risk of a cadre of Boy Scouts and their leader. I am grateful for their encouragement and the fun of working together.

Finally, for her putting up with writing in my cave for hours, the encouragement to share the adventure, and suggestions along the way, my wife Marianne has contributed greatly to telling the story. I am grateful. We have laughed together and sometimes shaken our heads, wondering at the antics of boys so long ago and how the seven of us somehow survived.

CPSIA information can be obtained at www.ICGtesting.com
Printed in the USA
BVOW08s2358060416

443292BV00001B/6/P